BEYOND DUALITY:

The Art of Transcendence

Other Titles From New Falcon Publications

Undoing Yourself With Energized Meditation
Secrets of Western Tantra
    By Christopher S. Hyatt, Ph.D.
The Enochian World of Aleister Crowley
    By Aleister Crowley, L. M. DuQuette, and C. S. Hyatt
Rebels & Devils: A Psychology of Liberation
    Editor C.S. Hyatt with contributions by William S. Burroughs, et. al.
Pacts With The Devil
    By S. Jason Black and Christopher S. Hyatt, Ph.D.
Buddhism and Jungian Psychology
Catholicism and Jungian Psychology
    By J. Marvin Spiegelman, Ph.D.
Cosmic Trigger III: My Life After Death
Prometheus Rising
The New Inquisition
    By Robert Anton Wilson
Equinox of the Gods
Eight Lectures on Yoga
Gems From the Equinox
    By Aleister Crowley
Neuropolitique
Info-Psychology
The Game of Life
    By Timothy Leary, Ph.D.
Zen Without Zen Masters
    By Camden Benares
The Complete Golden Dawn System of Magic
    By Israel Regardie
Carl Sagan and Immanuel Velikovsky
    By Charles Ginenthal
Soul Magic: Understanding Your Journey
    By Katherine Torres, Ph.D.
The Mysteries Revealed
    By Andrew Schneider
Astrology and Consciousness: The Wheel of Light
    By Rio Olesky
Metaskills: The Spiritual Art of Therapy
    By Amy Mindell, Ph.D.

And to get your free catalog of *all* of our titles, write to:

New Falcon Publications (Catalog Dept.)
1739 East Broadway Road, Suite 1-277
Tempe, Arizona 85282 U.S.A

BEYOND DUALITY:
The Art of Transcendence

By

Laurence Galian

1995
NEW FALCON PUBLICATIONS
TEMPE, ARIZONA U.S.A.

International Standard Book Number: 1-56184-076-9

First Falcon Edition 1995

Cover art and Illustrations by Denise Cuttitta

The paper used in this publication meets the minimum require-ments of the American National Standard for Permanence of Paper for Printed Library Materials Z39.48-1984

Address all inquiries to:
New Falcon Publications
1739 East Broadway Road Suite 1-277
Tempe, Arizona 85282 U.S.A.
(or)
1605 East Charleston Blvd.
Las Vegas, NV 89104 U.S.A.

Dedicated to the loving memory of my beloved mother
Lillian Coffey Gagliano,
January 16, 1922 - October 12, 1994

For when all is equilibrated, when all is beheld without all, there is joy, joy, joy that is but one facet of a diamond, every other facet whereof is more joyful than joy itself. —Aleister Crowley

The key to the manifestation of all things through the differentiation into pairs of Opposites and their union in a Third. —Dion Fortune

Any technology that does not account for both elements of its component dualities will ultimately fail. —Stephen Mace

Your desires shall become flesh, your dreams reality and no fear shall alter it one whit. —A. O. Spare

Experience physically the tidal-tug of the amplitudes. —Philip K. Dick

ACKNOWLEDGMENTS

Thank you to the following friends and colleagues for their support, both of this book and of my work in general: Charles Rizzo who has been my closest friend and comrade, Mary Holly, Linda Crenwelge, and M. Crimson.

My eternal love and gratitude to Josephine Ufert who gave me the most precious gift, and to her husband Frank and son Karl.

I wish to express my appreciation to Denise Cuttitta, the Cover Artist and Illustrator, for her extraordinary artistic vision.

The creative ideas of Denney Colt have been invaluable. I especially want to thank Teresa Nolan for her invaluable and expert proofreading and editing of the book.

Finally, thanks to Nicholas Tharcher of New Falcon Publications for his advice, assistance, encouragement and expertise.

TABLE OF CONTENTS

Part III

PREFACE

This is a book of magick. There is a magickal power that arises through the reconciliation of duality. You can use this power to help you manifest your personal goals. Herein are contained the arts and techniques of utilizing this state of magickal equilibrium for spiritual growth, personal power, and success. Within this book "buried treasure" is brought to light. I have unearthed for the reader magickal concepts that have long lain hidden, unused, and unappreciated in the metaphysical literature. The theories and methods of ancient sages and occultists are introduced in a straightforward manner that is clear and useful to the modern magickian.

In this comprehensive guide not only do I bring these concepts into the light, but I design magickal methods to help you to have the full and abundant life you deserve.

This book is specifically directed towards practitioners of the Western Mystery Traditions, Qabalah, Chaos Magick, Ceremonial Magick, Wicca, and Shamanism who have had an introduction to the principles of magick and who want to expand upon their knowledge of this field.

When I first set out to write this book I intended to write a book on the subject of imagistic magick (otherwise known as "Creative Visualization"). However as the work evolved it became clear to me that what I had to say embraced a much wider, but interconnected, range of subject matter.

While setting my thoughts down on paper I realized that I was exploring the very mysteries of the process of creation itself. Over time this work became an investigation into the very nature of reality and the precise techniques that will enable you, the reader, to manifest what you want *in* that reality.

Herein you will be introduced to a complete system of magick that I call *The Way of Power*. *The Way of Power* is a series of magickal techniques and practices. This system is a clear and objective method for achieving your goals in life. Here you will discover the True Keys to Unlocking the Storehouses of the Universe!

The Way of Power is a system of magick intended to help you restructure your beliefs about your reality. *The Way of Power* will restructure *you* if you let it. A different person will finish reading this book than the one who started reading it.

I wish to acknowledge some of the people (living and deceased) whose lives have greatly influenced my own:

Douglas Adams
Ahkenaton
Aisha, Upon Her Be Peace
Amergin
Apollonius of Tyana
Clive Barker
Sheikh Tosun Bayrak al-Jerrahi al-Halveti
Ingmar Bergman
Botticelli
Albert Camus
Jean Cocteau
Robert Steven Connett
Tom Cowan
Aleister Crowley
Sri Swami Dayananda Saraswati
Charles DeLint
James Gerard DeMartini
Philip K. Dick
Linda Folorio
Sigmund Freud
Dion Fortune
Robert Goddard
Kenneth Grant
Paul Gustav Doré

Hermann Hesse
Jesus of Nazareth
Joan of Arc
Omar Kayyam
Alexie Kondratiev
Lao-tzu
Gunnel Lindblom
Morgan Llewellyn
Stephen Mace
Leo Martello
John Matthews
Terence McKenna
Gustav Moreau
Kaledon Naddair
Nietzsche
Nijinsky
Anaïs Nin
Anthony Norvel
Sheikh Nur al-Jerrahi al-Halveti
Hazreti Pir Nureddin Jerrahi, The Axis of the Sufis
Hazreti Muzaffer Ozak al-Jerrahi al-Halveti
Wilhelm Reich
Jalal al-Din Rumi

Austin Osman Spare	J.R.R. Tolkein
Jean Paul Sartre	Liv Ullmann
Rachel Pollack	Richard Wagner
The Prophet Mohammed, The	Barbara Walker
Pride of the Universe	Ophiel
Ayn Rand	Wallace D. Wattles
Israel Regardie	Racquel Welch
Rudolph Steiner	Robert Anton Wilson
R.J. Stewart	Yung-chia

Finally, there is one being, Peace and Blessings be Upon Him, who must be recognized, I am referring to Hermes Trismegistus (Thrice Great Hermes) the first framer of this philosophy.

* * *

Beyond Duality: The Art of Transcendence is the result of a long evolutionary process in my soul. I discovered creative imagination in 1977 but for quite a while I experienced only sporadic results when I employed its methods. Perhaps you have had the same experience when you tried visualization...some goals materializing within hours, while other goals continuing to remain elusive.

There was definitely something to this system of magick—creative imagination worked, it just didn't work consistently or reliably. Sometimes it produced change in my environment, sometimes it didn't. I knew I didn't yet have all the answers. I was getting only unpredictable and partial results; I wanted to produce a more precise effect. Yet I blamed myself. I put the book down and thought "It must be my fault. I must not be visualizing long enough, or vividly enough."

Over time it occurred to me that the books gave good, but *incomplete*, information. Years of metaphysical research and practice have revealed to me that there is a *missing* factor in almost all books of magick on the market! This glaring omission renders all these books practically use-less. Creative imagination books, even the best, have left out an extremely important spiritual concept which is absolutely necessary to make visualization work on a steady basis. I learned about creative imagination "the hard way"—by doing what *doesn't* work. In the process of manifesting my life goals, I have discovered what *does* work.

This new work reveals this overlooked element and gives *precise* directions on its utilization.

Some of this knowledge was known prior to the Egyptian age. For centuries observers of human nature have sought the hidden patterns and webs of forces that lie behind our behavior. These men and women, who dared peer into these hidden realms, were called "Initiates" for they have been *initiated* into the mysteries of existence.

Initiates often wrote down their wisdom in a coded or 'veiled' style. Others encoded their wisdom in pictorial form as in the Tarot Cards, the Hindu Yantras, or as in the Hebrew Tree of Life. Additional wisdom was interwoven into myth and fairy tales. But these "maps of consciousness" have been *deciphered* by only a select few mystics and practicing occultists who have had the ability to "read between the lines."

As you may know, if you look up the definition of the term "occult" you will discover that it simply means: concealed or hidden. In *Beyond Duality: The Art of Transcendence* I have lifted the concealing veil. I have removed all the mumbo-jumbo, the obfuscation, and the endless rambling contained in the works of occult authors. This book exposes the very essence of their teachings.

Several concepts will be introduced, including the magickal heart of the book *"The Triangle of Manifestation ."* Furthermore, we will explore Sigils, Talismans, and many other Meta-Programming, Cyber-Shamanic, and Chaos Magickal techniques.

This information has never before been revealed to the public in this form! This book will teach you how to communicate and impress your will upon the Spirit Realms thereby causing certain subtle shifts in the operative paradigms, which in turn will modify your environment.

To create miracles, one must become a miracle! Accordingly, this work helps you to explore issues involved in becoming a whole person, and in realizing that you are a star. Effective magick is not so much based on *what* you know, but on what you *are*.

* * *

Throughout this book you will see the word "MAGIC" spelled as "MAGICK" with a "K." The "K" distinguishes Magick as a path of soul-development as distinct from slight of hand or illusion as practiced on the stage.

May Isis part her Veil for you through the words of this book. Come, let us travel to the point of infinite possibility.

> Laurence Galian
> December 28, 1994
> 10:14 AM
> Hempstead, New York

PART I

UPS AND DOWNS

The teacher brought the student to a flight of stairs and bade him ascend the staircase. The student did as he was told and when he was at the top, his teacher beckoned him down. When the student had descended the steps the teacher sent the student back up and then down the stairs several more times.

Several times the student wondered to himself while doing this exercise if there was any point in it at all, or if maybe his teacher harbored some secret desire to see the student exhaust himself by climbing steps.

Finally the teacher asked the student: "So now what do you know about the staircase?" The student thought for a moment and began tentatively: "It has ten steps."

The Teacher remarked: "Well said. What else can you tell me about this staircase?"

The Student answered: "The staircase moves me from one place to another."

"So, it's an 'up' staircase?"

"Well, that depends on which direction you're heading."

"So are you saying that it is both an 'up' and a 'down' staircase depending on your point of view?"

"Yes, it was 'up' while I was traveling up and 'down' when I was traveling down.'

"Well then, tell me which is the superior step."

The Student thought long and hard at this question because he was sure it was a trick question.

"I think *all* of them are important, sir."

"Are you certain it's not that last step all the way up top?"

For a moment the student thought that he should agree with his teacher, but then decided to be true to his own perceptions.

"I perceive that no one step is any more important than any other. The first step is just as necessary as the last step."

"Good, very good. They are all interdependent upon one another."

The Teacher continued: "One step can not be superior to any other step, for all are absolutely necessary, absolutely essential if one wishes to have a complete staircase."

The analogy of a staircase can be useful in understanding many situations in life. We perceive levels of learning, vibration, and experience in the people and events around us. But note, each and every level is as necessary as another to the complete and effective functioning of the whole.

The idea of "staircase" involves an interconnected and interdependent whole. The staircase simply IS.

VIBRATING UNIVERSE

Hermetics teaches us that *all the universe is in vibration*, from the lowest planes to the highest planes. Just like a piano, being played by a concert pianist, vibrates from its lowest notes, to its highest.

For too long spiritual writers and thinkers have portrayed a universe that is hierarchical, the bottom being bad/evil/materialistic, and the top being exalted/good/spiritual. For many of us, our religious upbringing consisted of learning the physical body was "sinful" and that the only thing of value in a human being was the soul or spirit.

Unfortunately, the echoes of that body/soul dichotomy are still found in the writings of some modern metaphysical thinkers. They are fond of talking about "raising one's vibrations," as if being on the twelfth floor of a building was superior to being on the first floor! If that were the case, elevators would be holy objects and we'd all have achieved illumination by now.

Let's again consider the concert pianist. As we listen to him or her play, we are aware that a musical composition is a vehicle by which composers express their experience. Our bodies, too, are vehicles of expression. They are the expression of the spirit-world.

Now the piece of music isn't the composer, it has a life of its own. Yet when you hear the music you say "that's Beethoven," or "that's Bach," or "that's Wagner." You recognize the composer in the piece!

The composer's essence is mystically intertwined with his or her composition. As a master-piece of music wears the stamp of genius, we wear a "stamp of spirit-force."

And what is Spirit? It is US! We wear the imprint of our own FUTURE! Our future selves are calling out to us, echoing within us.

Let's get back to the concert pianist... Looking at the piano, can we say that a musical note 3 octaves below middle C is inferior to a note 3 octaves above? The lower tones of the bass are just as necessary as the higher tones of the treble.

Music exists simultaneously in a state of creation and dissolution. At the very moment it is created it also gives up its life. It is a beautiful expression of the nature of the universe, like the candle flame which always exists at that perfect balance point, the flame is always being born out of the Unmanifest. As the Great Hindu God, Krishna, says "I make and unmake this universe."

POWER CENTERS

The universe is wholly interconnected. Recent scientific research has confirmed this ancient magickal way of viewing the world. Its interconnectedness can be likened to a giant Persian or Oriental carpet.

Reflect on how this beautiful middle-eastern carpet is full of vibrant color and design; then, consider the way that the threads are woven together to create this work of *ART*... every thread interdependent upon the other.

The same principle of interconnectedness holds true for a good pot of stew. All the flavors blend together to create something which is greater than the sum of its parts.

Our lives are a continuous interplay of energies between us and this web of life with which we are interconnected. Our every thought affects the web. *The Way of Power* uses this knowledge to work *with* the web to empower our magick!

Within the web there are energy centers to which we can attune ourselves. Our goal is to harmonize with these localities. Different spiritual teachers have given various names to these power centers—vortexes, power-spots, nature devas, animal totems, WatchTowers, Gods and Goddesses, archetypes, and consciousness resonance matrices.

By whatever name they may be called, these energy centers within the web are great untapped wells of highly organized power. From these centers you can channel energy to manifest your goals using *The Way of Power* outlined in this book.

THE SACRED BODY

The body is and isn't the person. What is meant by this? Simply that as human beings we have a dual nature that must be honored and integrated. The seed of the Spirit is contained within the Body, just as the seed of the Body is contained within the Spirit. G. K. Chesterton wrote: "Lo, blessed are our ears for they have heard; Yea, blessed are our eyes for they have seen." We must thank, acknowledge, and honor our sense organs for the joy of experience they bring to us.

The body is the MANIFEST; the UNMANIFEST is the spirit. The manifest and the unmanifest both are *equally* valid, important, and necessary. It's so simple. You don't have to go any further than your own nose or your weekly bowling night to find God. To paraphrase the Koran "Allah is closer than your jugular vein."

Let us once and for all get rid of the archaic and patriarchal notion that the universe operates like some kind of medieval castle in which there is a hierarchical chain of command extending from the King all the way down to the Serf.

We don't so much have LEVELS as ASPECTS. It might be a lot more healthy to think of ourselves as having various aspects rather than hierarchies of levels.

"Levels" imply that parts of our being are "better-than" others. "Aspects" implies an interconnected whole. We have biologic aspects of our natures that must be understood and embraced. For they can be the direct means to influence the spiritual aspects and thereby produce CHANGE on the physical plane!

Is walking slowly somehow inferior to walking quickly?

25

INTERDEPENDENCY

Like steps of a staircase, and notes on a piano, each part MUST be present for the whole to function properly. Just because one plane vibrates at a lower frequency than another plane, the former is not inferior to the latter. Bass tones vibrate at a lower frequency than treble tones, yet *both* tones are essential to the total effect of the music.

The physical universe is sacred and just as "spiritual" as any "soul" that priests and theologians might think up.

Consider an ordinary flashlight battery. Look at or visualize one. Can you imagine if the battery only had a positive end, but not a negative end? What good would it be if it had only a positive pole, but not a negative pole? It wouldn't be functional. It wouldn't work. It wouldn't even *be* a battery. Most importantly of all, from a magickal point of view, it wouldn't be *charged* !

Every substance in this universe is just as significant as any other substance. We miss the quality of a substance because of *our* sense limitations, not the substances. Take the case of the mineral *Cesium*. To the naked eye Cesium appears to be a soft, silvery-white metallic substance that is liquid at room temperature. Our eyes cannot perceive that the atoms of a *Cesium* molecule vibrate at over five billion cycles a second!

There is so much in this wide universe that is unseen, unheard, unperceived by our senses, yet nonetheless exists. It is a medieval notion that nothing exists which we cannot perceive. We human beings have room in ourselves to admit to experiences which do not fit into the scientist's test-tube. Whole realms of existence interpenetrate the reality which is accessible to us through our bodily senses.

There exists a kind of arrogance among scholars and scientists. If a theorist's ideas do not fit neatly into the scientific paradigm, then those theories are regarded laughable and pathetic by the scientific community. Why?

It is only through *questioning authority* that humanity makes advances in its collective wisdom. Rather than being laughed at, *renegades* of science should be praised for blazing new trails in human consciousness. It takes courage to look for that which human beings are unaware. These cosmic scouts are the brave ones!

At present, some astronomers are exploring the possibility of an *unknown* force in the universe. These same astronomers think that, besides gravity, there is a force of which humankind is unaware and which is responsible for the distribution of matter throughout the cosmos.

Some astronomers and physicists are now speculating that the great expanding fire-ball of the universe is actually a huge, growing *fractal* !

Never let anyone insinuate that because your thoughts are those of the poet or dreamer, that they are in any way inferior to the down-to-earth concerns of the business of science. Our world is getting more spiritual and magickal moment by moment!

THE TWO-WAY FLOW OF THE UNIVERSE

The universe flows in two directions simultaneously. This flow is comparable to Alternating Current. Electronics teaches us that the flow of electricity in the wires in our walls, in our appliances, and so forth, actually changes direction and polarity at a rapid rate. This rapid changing of direction or polarity is what 'alternates' in Alternating Current. The rate of this alternation is sixty cycles per second, which is to say that the current changes its *charge* back and forth from positive to negative sixty times each second.

From the rapid oscillation of Positive to Negative and back again, comes the powerful flow of Alternating Current. If only one polarity were used the strength of the current would be vastly reduced. Think of how this balancing of energies can make *your* magickal work even more powerful!

In the cosmos we meet two chief forces: spirit and matter. How does the *Two-Way Flow of the Universe* manifest in the cosmos at large? Spirit continuously manifests matter, and matter continuously manifests spirit. From out of the spirit worlds matter is continuously being spewed forth. This mystery is like a great ejaculation; the divine convulses in a state of ecstasy and produces matter...and then matter answers as humankind has sex and in the moment of sexual orgasm calls out to God. At the same time, without matter there would be no spirit.

There is a saying in the occult community that goes: The Gods need us as much as we need the Gods! We, by our

very human and physical natures, permit the Spirit World
to Exist! We emanate from our bodies this Spirit World.
This reciprocal operation of the cosmos is very important
to remember in your magickal workings.

The Divine would be unknown if it wasn't for us. It
would still be a *Great Unknown Mystery*. We make it come
alive as we enter into relationship with it. Our bodies are
the *expression* of the Divine. This fact might cause us to
pause and ask ourselves 'So who is there really to pray to?'
Those individuals who say "God is Dead" are wrong, they
just don't realize that their mundane bodies give rise to the
Divine; they only need to look at their physical forms and
they will see God.

At this point I want to pause a moment and describe
what I mean by the word spiritual. The spiritual realm is
not some insubstantial, airy, ethereal place. The Spiritual
Realms are in a way *more* real and concrete than the
physical world.

The Spirit World is filled with power, substantiality, and
presence. I recommend you work on changing your consciousness with regard to Spirit and begin to see Spirit as
the *Power Matrix* from which the physical world manifests.
As a person's spirit eyes start to open he or she will begin
to realize that he/she has had it backwards all along… The
Physical World is thin and gossamer compared to the
Spirit Realm.

This Universe needs *all* its aspects to *Be* a Universe. Take
one aspect away, and the wall comes tumbling down. Puff,
no more Universe!

THE NATURAL KINGDOM

Nature is not always "fair" as some people would define the term. Some of the laws of nature call for destruction. Part of the natural ecology of animal life is that animals are killed and eaten by other animals every day.

Even in your own back-yard, feline sadism is displayed in a good-natured old tom "playing" with a mouse. There is not so much justice as there is balance in nature.

There are earth-quakes and there are rainbows. There are tornadoes and there are sunsets. There are thorns and there are roses.

Frankly, I've never seen a moral lion. Lions must kill their prey. The animals which are killed obviously do suffer as they die. We must not fall into a comfortable *illusion* of a pastoral and untroubled natural world. One of the first rules of the Magickian is to OBSERVE carefully and dispassionately his or her environment. Notice the details around you, not just the pleasant parts, but include ALL that is dark and terrible in nature.

Since we humans are part of the natural world, it should not be a shock that a combination of pleasing and displeasing events would occur in our personal lives. It may not be realistic to expect smooth sailing all the time. Perhaps a more healthy view would be to take into account THE TWO-WAY FLOW OF THE UNIVERSE and develop the skill of walking between opposites.

THE FLIP SIDE

Am I saying then, that we must invite into our lives pain, sorrow, and suffering...all the negatives? No! But we must *acknowledge* that just as a shield has two sides (as do coins, bed-sheets, and pages) so too does the Universe have two sides. Ultimately there is really no way to say one side is better than the other, since both sides emanate from the Ultimate Reality.

Even in the language of the Christian religion, "evil" is necessary to show God's love. For example, the Father's Son is tortured and crucified on a Cross for our "sins." If there were no "sins" there would be no need for an atonement and a crucifixion.

Consider this: the Christ's message was to preach love. If Satan is Christ's *enemy* then it is only through a profound love of that foe that enmity is reconciled. To love someone means to accept them in their entirety.

In the Jewish religion there is no devil per se, rather Satan is the "adversary." He is there to test the Chosen People. He enjoys audiences with Yahweh. Satan gets to frequently converse with and challenge the Almighty. Thus, through the effects of the Dark Side (in this case Satan) the individual is proven a faithful believer.

In Islam and especially Sufism, the devil "Iblis" enjoys some special attention and honor. Mohammed, May Peace Be Upon Him, said: "The throne of Iblis is upon the ocean and he sends detachments in order to put people to trial..."

It is in the very nature of physical plane existence that the Ultimate Reality must manifest in a simultaneously positive and negative polarity.

First, we admit to ourselves that the dark side, the "shadow" side of life, is a reality and then, we embrace the Dark and *integrate* it within ourselves. The Dark is only dangerous when it is ignored and repressed! It is through the *encounter* with the *opposite* that real achievement can arise.

So, our goal is not to remove "evil," but to equilibrate unbalanced thoughts. Thoughts that remain lopsided, in other words, not confronted with their opposites, are *distorted thoughts*. Distorted thoughts give a false view of reality and thereby confuse any magickal working we may attempt. When we equilibrate unbalanced thoughts we achieve an *integration* within ourselves and we create a *coherent self*!

I would submit that what we term "evil" is not a lower vibration but a state of turmoil produced from damned-up energy fields inside us. When we block the free flow of sexual energy through repression, guilt and fear, the sex energy must find some outlet. Neurosis is the result of damned-up sexual energy.

The consequence is that the sex energy expresses itself inappropriately and in twisted ways. Or else if it is so damned up that it cannot get out in any way, sex energy will begin to fester and cause all sorts of diseases and mental illnesses. Sexual energy deprived of its normal target is forced to seek fulfillment elsewhere.

It is the Magickian's task to transform his or her mind. You can transform your mind in many ways. When the teacher utters: "Wake Up!" the teacher is attempting to rouse up your Self from its lethargy.

One time-tested way of doing this is to transform your being by *energizing* it. You can energize your being through the method of synthesizing opposites.

By synthesizing contradictions you begin to achieve a unity of being and purpose. Unity arises through the equilibration of all opposites into the point of transcendence. You then become a lightening bolt of power, transcending all contradictions. Your total power becomes greater than the sum of your parts. This is the Great

Alchemical Marriage that is spoken of in the ancient texts: the annihilation of two ingredients at the birth of a third.

BALANCE

Everything must be *balanced* in this Universe. You can't go very long in one direction before the pendulum starts to swing back in the opposite direction. This isn't just a spiritual principle, it manifests every day on the physical, emotional and mental planes of existence.

A plane flying east from New York, provided it has enough fuel, will eventually end up back in New York. At a certain point on the globe it ceases going away from New York and starts heading back towards New York. That's the nature of living on a globe. It could not be otherwise. The Globe, Our Mother Earth, completely balances the forces of East-West, and North-South.

We would be wise to look to nature to learn the deepest secrets of esoteric wisdom. Night and Day, Summer and Winter, Life and Death, Male and Female, all opposites manifest and are balanced in the world.

No doubt, many of you have seen the Yin-Yang symbol (☯). This symbol perfectly expresses the divine interplay of forces of negative and positive polarity.

When meditating upon this symbol one first sees that it is a circle. All is contained within that circle. The circle represents the Ultimate Reality.

Think of a wheel. The center of the wheel is always at rest. The center *balances all opposites*. In fact, all the opposites in equilibrium make possible the *idea* of the wheel.

As you gaze at the Yin/Yang symbol, you perceive interweaved light and dark areas. These areas express the coupled nature of the universe—the day and the night, the light and the dark, the summer and the winter—each aspect of the cosmos coupled with its opposite.

AN EXPLOSION OF ENERGY

"She loves me; she loves me not; she loves me; she loves me not." Remember this game from childhood? How many of us have actually tried this? Believe it or not, this children's amusement has a basis in reality. It is the remnant of an occult mystery.

When we chant "She loves me, she loves me not..." we are balancing one thought with its exact, polar opposite. We are deliberately setting-up a contradiction in the mind. We put the mind on overload.

The result is that the mind cannot satisfy both these two contradictory concepts, and hence reconciles them. In the process of reconciliation, a kind of energy discharge occurs. At the moment the two statements are fused there is released an outburst of energy. This is exactly what happens when matter and anti-matter are brought together. The duality is nullified and power is released. This undifferentiated power can in turn be used magickally.

HORUS AND SET

The two ancient Egyptian Gods Ra-Hoor-Khuit and Hoor-paar-kraat, otherwise known as Horus and Set, are *identical*. Horus was the child of Isis and Osiris, he is called *Heru* "The Hawk of Heaven" or Hero. He represents the conquest of the sun over the darkness.

Set is the brother of Osiris, who slew his brother and is called the "Bringer of Confusion," "Agent of Chaos," "and "Champion of Darkness." Horus sought to avenge his father's death by fighting with Set and overcoming him.

Yet, in the sense that any idea can exist only by virtue of the contradiction contained within it, the two Gods Horus and Set are really two poles of one Ultimate Reality.

I recommend that you meditate for a while on the occult maxim: "I am because I am not." Explore the discrepancy and the insanity of this statement. Delight in the contradiction. Then enter into the Silence of Transcendence. The *silence* is the key to the understanding of the relationship of Horus and Set.

EQUILIBRIUM

There is a state of awareness in the Universe that the awakened ones possess. In this state of awareness, all opposites unite: dark and light, day and night, pleasure and pain, hot and cold, and so forth.

There are myriad ancient sayings which express this view, such as:

"There is a reverse side to every shield."
"Everything is and isn't at the same time."
"All truths are but half truths.
"There are two sides to everything."
"I am because I am not."
"Form is nothing but void, void is nothing but form."

Opposites are in fact only two extremes of the same thing! A coin might have two sides, but they are the two sides of ONE coin. It is by arriving at this mountain top level of realization that enables you to manifest your goals through *The Way of Power* .

An ancient and wise saying of Hermetic Science says: "As above so below, and so below as above." The "above" has been called the Macrocosm, or the Larger View of the Universe, the "below" has been called the Microcosm, or the Personal View of the Universe. We human beings are the entire cosmos in miniature. When we magickally work on ourselves, we are simultaneously magickally affecting our environment.

The expression "Man was made in the image and likeness of God," illuminates this concept of Macrocosm and Microcosm. *Human beings need the Gods as much as the Gods need human beings.*

THE INHERENT CONTRADICTION

The secret to *The Way of Power* lies in the concept of *The Equilibrium*. The entire universe exists in a state of balance.

To maintain this state of equilibrium every idea in the universe must hold within itself its own contradiction.

Consider the matter of love. There is a contradictory force contained within love. We are not referring here to hate, which would be love's opposite, but we are referring to the opposite contained within love.

What would this contradictory force be? How would it manifest? A perfect example can be seen in the concept of "tough love."

What is "tough love?" This is a special modern technique taught by therapists, counselors, and those experts in family dynamics.

The practice of "tough love" can best be explained through illustration. Take the case of a woman who has a son in his twenties that refuses to work. He just sits around all day and watches television. Now one day the mother comes home after a session with the family counselor and announces to her son that he must get a job or else she will be forced to ask him to leave the house. Weeks pass and the boy doesn't get work; he's still watching "talk-shows" when the mother arrives home in the evening.

At this point the woman has another session with her family counselor and, when she arrives home she tells the young man to leave the house and not to come back until he has obtained work.

Now to an outside observer, this action of the mother may seem cruel and heartless, in other words, casting her son out into the world without so much as a job or money in his pocket. Yet, to the discerning witness of this drama, the mother's actions are nothing other than *altruistic love*. For she is forcing her son to "wake up and smell the coffee!" She is, in reality, *helping* her son to assume responsibility for his life. Although seemingly cruel, she is actually deeply loving him.

Thus we see that when an individual practices "tough love" he or she sometimes has to cause pain to the loved one. The individual sometimes must force the loved one to go without food, housing, affection, and so on, to teach him or her a greater lesson in love. In fact, in order to truly love them, the *only* choice in such situations is "tough love."

What in other contexts might be construed as *hate*, when viewed in the context of "tough love," is seen as nothing other than *love*. *The secret of* The Triangle of Manifestation *is that we equilibrate our desired thought by thinking of its inherent contradiction.*

PRACTICAL APPLICATION

Let us now create *"The Triangle of Manifestation."* First, we picture in our mind an Equilateral Triangle. We begin by concentrating on what we do want. If our goal is to manifest love in our life, we would begin by thinking of ourselves being in love. This thought of being in love creates the first point or bottom left angle of the Triangle.

Then our next step would be to think of the apparent contradiction of being in love. For example, we would think of ourselves practicing "tough-love." This now creates the second point or bottom right angle at the base of the triangle.

When the two thoughts are thus balanced, both thoughts accelerate together (like opposite poles of two magnets attracting one another) and are *immediately annihilated and destroyed*, creating a magickal THIRD POINT OF TRANSCENDENCE (or *Point of Infinite Possibility*) at the top point of the triangle.

A VISUAL METAPHOR

Something similar to *The Triangle of Manifestation* occurs in the process of eyesight. Think how we use two eyes in the operation of seeing. The first eyeball delivers its information to the brain, while simultaneously the second eyeball delivers its information, but from a slightly different perspective to the brain. At which point and time, the two divergent "views" are magickally synthesized in the brain to create a "Third" view.

The resultant "3-D" experience of eyesight *is* the Third Point of Transcendence. Two pictures (from the right eye and from the left eye) combine in the brain and are synthesized into a Third picture in 3-D! The stereoscopic visual experience is greater than the sum of its parts.

With two eyes we experience depth and perspective; yet, if we only saw out of one eyeball we would see only a flat and two-dimensional world.

THE TRIANGLE OF MANIFESTATION

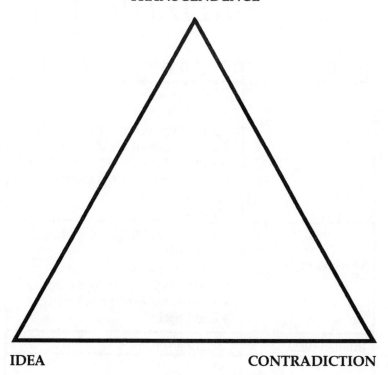

TRANSCENDENCE

IDEA

CONTRADICTION

EXAMPLES OF IDEAS AND THE CONTRADICTIONS CONTAINED THEREIN

IDEA	CONTRADICTION THEREIN
Love	Tough-Love * * * * * * * * * * * * * * * * * * * A parent teaching a child to ride a bike—the parent needs to risk letting the child fall in order for the child to learn to ride the bike * * * * * * * * * * * * * * * * * * * Self-discipline
Movement	A flower unfolding *slower* than the eye can see * * * * * * * * * * * * * * * * * * * A stage magician doing a card trick *faster* than the eye can see (sleight of hand tricks)
Intelligence	Common sense
Happiness	Tears of joy * * * * * * * * * * * * * * * * * * Bittersweetness

Strength	Discretion is the better part of valor
	* * * * * * * * * * * * * * * * * * * *
	Walking away from a no win situation
	* * * * * * * * * * * * * * * * * * * *
	Turning the other cheek
	* * * * * * * * * * * * * * * * * * * *
	Walking softly but carrying a big stick
Health	A healing crisis
	* * * * * * * * * * * * * * * * * * * *
	Chemotherapy
	* * * * * * * * * * * * * * * * * * * *
	Surgery
	* * * * * * * * * * * * * * * * * * * *
	Radiation
	* * * * * * * * * * * * * * * * * * * *
	Amputation to save a life
Pleasure	S&M
	* * * * * * * * * * * * * * * * * * * *
	Enjoying tart foods, pungent cheeses, hot peppers, and so forth
Freedom	Any choice
	* * * * * * * * * * * * * * * * * * * *
	To get married
	* * * * * * * * * * * * * * * * * * * *
	Have a family
	* * * * * * * * * * * * * * * * * * * *
	Take a particular job
Truthfulness	Tact
	* * * * * * * * * * * * * * * * * * * *
	Prudence

Intelligibility	A document written in code
Marriage	A secret marriage * * * * * * * * * * * * * * * * * * * An elopement * * * * * * * * * * * * * * * * * * * An arranged marriage
Travel	Astral travel * * * * * * * * * * * * * * * * * * Watching a travelogue
Wisdom	When you are privy to special information
Joy	Bittersweet * * * * * * * * * * * * * * * * * * * Nostalgia
Youth	A mature child
Hardness	Bend like a reed in the wind
Getting Attention, Being Noticed	When a teacher speaks very quietly to get the class's attention.
Being Respected	When someone admires you from afar
Wealth	Rich in spirit * * * * * * * * * * * * * * * * * * Someone who's won the lottery but doesn't know it yet * * * * * * * * * * * * * * * * * * * Someone who's inherited a fortune who isn't aware of it
Light	Blinding light
Life	Sleep

STEP BY STEP

You can use the examples given above to create your "Triangle" or you can think up instances of contradictory forces yourself.

Remember: do not think of the opposite...think of the contradiction inherent in the force that you want to draw into your life. This will take some thinking, but the energy you expend in figuring out the inherent contradiction, actually is part of the process of creating a paradigm shift in your life.

A helpful formula to discover the contradictory force inherent in any idea is as follows: First think of your desired goal. Ask yourself: "What concept or idea would be expressed through the materialization of my goal?"

For instance, if you were sick and wanted to get well your goal—getting well—would give expression to the concept of *health*. "Health" would be your first point of the triangle.

You would then ask yourself: "What is the contradictory idea contained in the concept of health?" You might reflect on how a physician, in order to help an individual heal themselves, will sometimes cut into the individual's body and perform procedures which in any other context would be considered life-threatening.

Or you might think of how cancer patients choose to take toxic poisons in the form of chemotherapy into their blood-streams in order to restore their bodies to health. Cancer patients thereby save their lives by putting themselves in jeopardy through the injection of deadly chemicals into the bloodstream. They are doing something which in any other context would be construed as self-destructive, yet in this context is highly beneficial.

THE SECRET FORMULA

A helpful technique to assist you in discovering the contradiction *contained* in your desired goal is to use the following formula: When does (*positive*) appear to be (*negative*)?

In the "positive" blank we would fill-in our desired outcome, and in the "negative" blank we would fill-in the opposite of what we want to achieve. In the instance of health, we would come out with something like the following sentence: When does health appear to be sickness?

WHY DO WE NEED TO EQUILIBRATE?

In balancing each desired goal with the contradiction contained therein, we cause our thought to be re-born at the very point from which all creation manifests.

When we balance each thought with the opposite contained within it, we cause our wish to be implanted within the fertile divine matrix. This divine matrix exists at the junction of the twofold movements. At this junction there are no opposites. Our wish manifests as a reverberation of the apex of the movement. This insures that the pendulum of polarity will not swing away from us and thereby take away our manifestation, for the idea behind the manifestation will be anchored in non-duality and balanced on both points of the triangle.

PART II

THE HEGELIAN DIALECTIC

The resulting materialization of balanced visualization is often neither the initial desire nor the contradiction contained within, but instead a surpassing of the two. In philosophical terms this is known as the Hegelian dialectic: *Thesis-Antithesis-Synthesis*.

In magickal terms, Aleister Crowley illuminates this principle through the formula of I.A.O. "I" represents the Egyptian Goddess Isis. Isis represents the energy that flows at the beginning of any endeavor. She is connected symbolically to the Nile. She represents the virgin state of "the matter."

Next we come to the letter "A" which stands for Apophis, otherwise known as Set. Set is the deceiver. This is the time when enthusiasm and ardor at the beginning of the venture is replaced by the dull routine. The energetic forward *thrust* of the Isis Force meets up with the *inertia* of the Apophis Force. Apophis represents the opposing force of that which we are invoking.

Lastly, we come to the letter "O" which represents the Egyptian God, and brother-husband of Isis, "Osiris." Osiris was a mortal King, slain by Set who then rose from the dead. When Osiris rose from the dead, he became an Immortal God. Through his encounter with the Contradiction or Opposing Force (Set), Osiris becomes even greater than when he was a King. As Obi Wan says to Darth Vader in "Star Wars": "Cut me down and I will have more power than you can possibly imagine."

Therefore to sum up, when we only visualize the positive, we neglect the occult fact that eventually the universe will pull the pendulum in the opposite direction, thereby taking away our goal, *unless we do something to counteract the opposing force!* The solution is not to wage war upon the Opposing Force, not to exorcise it, banish it, or resist it, but to encounter it, and to find a way to integrate it into ourselves.

I A O

THE LEVELS OF A HUMAN BEING PICTURED AS AN ICEBERG

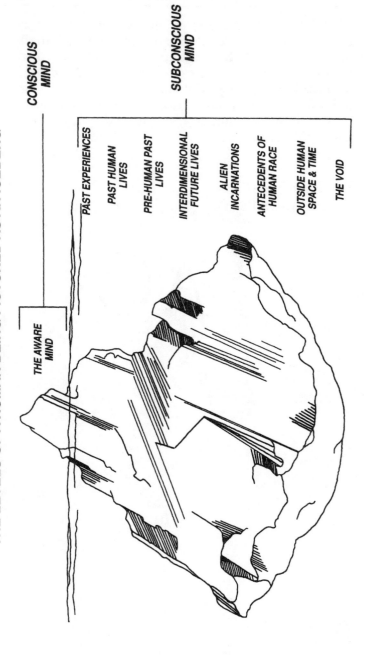

CONSCIOUS MIND

THE AWARE MIND

SUBCONSCIOUS MIND

PAST EXPERIENCES

PAST HUMAN LIVES

PRE-HUMAN PAST LIVES

INTERDIMENSIONAL FUTURE LIVES

ALIEN INCARNATIONS

ANTECEDENTS OF HUMAN RACE

OUTSIDE HUMAN SPACE & TIME

THE VOID

THE FORCE THAT MOVES MOUNTAINS

How can we use this awareness of *balance* to create desired change in our lives? First, we begin by looking at the subconscious, or the *dark* part of our minds. I call the subconscious the *dark* part because it is not consciously accessible; it is always watchful and present, yet it is hidden (occult) from our waking minds. In order to contact it we have to access an altered state of reality. In other words, to contact the subconscious we must go into a hypnotic trance, a shamanic trance, day-dream, or practice lucid dreaming.

Our beliefs about ourselves and our world are powerfully entrenched within the subconscious. It might be helpful when comparing the subconscious with the conscious mind to envision an iceberg.

As you are no doubt familiar, only a tiny portion of the entire iceberg shows above the water line, and the rest of the body of the iceberg *is under water*!

The tip of the iceberg can be compared to the conscious mind, and the huge mass under water can be likened to the *subconscious mind*.

Often we go through minutes, hours, and even days operating totally from our subconscious. We *think* we are in control, but the subconscious has established its *own* agenda and is really running the show. We are ASLEEP! *Walking Zombies*!

Many try affirmations as a way to change the subconscious programming. Yet, the subconscious will often "dig its feet in" harder when attempts are made to program it through verbal suggestions.

To cause change to happen a person needs a greater or bigger force than their own conscious mind to cause that pendulum to start swinging in the other direction. The person needs to embrace a bigger principle. That bigger principle is a Force existing all around you and within you, at your beck and call whenever you're ready to use it. It is THE ALL. The Eastern masters have called it the "Tao." It is the YANG and YIN of Creation. The AC and the DC. The LIGHT and the DARK. Both aspects of polarity present and in balance.

The techniques presented here utilize this force to empower and energize our efforts to change ourselves and our environment.

SYMBIONTS

We are symbionts, like 'Jadzia Dax' in *STAR TREK: DEEP SPACE NINE*. Our flesh depends as much on our spirit as our spirit depends on our flesh. Like it our not, one aspect can't exist without the other.

Spirit and Flesh are merely two sides of the same reality; they can be somewhat independently analyzed, but only by acknowledging our being as a *TOTALITY* can the full REALITY of our existence be known.

Many psychological studies have confirmed the interdependence of mind and body. We are not standing outside nature and observing it through a window. We ourselves are part of the nature we seek to describe. Our thoughts and perceptions can be greatly altered and distorted through bodily sickness and injury. These studies have not gone far enough, for not only is mind effected by the body, but the entire Spirit is changed in response to changes in the body. It is said that "You are what you eat." I'll go further and say: "You eat what you are." Our spiritual natures will give rise to how we manifest physically on the Earth plane, and hence will influence our choice of foods, our decision whether or not to consume animal flesh, and the way we take care of our bodies' health.

If you wonder about people with handicaps of the body or spirit, and those who suffer, I would reply that in a global sense we are not *individual* bodies or spirits, we animate ALL bodies and our bodies generate ALL spiritual reality.

I am every wo/man. Every wo/man is me. So each of us partakes of the reality of everyone else.

POLARITY TRANSCENDED

Life is one aspect of death and death is one aspect of life. Death and Life are merely two sides of the *same* coin. We who are living look in the direction of death and imagine it to be a state of bodilessness, in which we are pure spirit. Yet, the dead stare back and imagine life to be a state of enslavement in matter. Actually no one is completely dead or alive, the living are constantly carrying around the seed of death within themselves, while the dead ensoul a seed of life. Yung-chia, the Ch'an Buddhist teacher, declares: "What is real is void; what is void is real."

Transcend the opposites of death and life; find the Point of Singularity in which the two become One. Know that birth and death are the crest and trough of One Wave. We might begin to understand how this can be so if we cease thinking in a linear way. If our life and death can be seen as a simultaneity, then it is perfectly understandable how spirit and flesh can be so interdependent. In fact, when you pray or in any way attempt to contact spirit, you may very well be praying to your future self in its death manifestation.

THE NATURE OF REALITY

Visualize a piece of cotton cloth. What is the cloth made out of? Cotton fibers of course. Take the piece of cloth and unravel it and what happens to the cloth? Has it disappeared? What do you have left? Cotton fibers. But the cloth wasn't an illusion was it? Of course not. It was real. But where is it now? We are left with a lot of thread. Just cotton.

Now we can weave those threads together again and *voila*, the cloth reappears! Perhaps we can say the cloth reincarnated. *The cloth has its being in the cotton*. It manifests out of the cotton and returns back to cotton when it is unwound. Many cloths but just *one* cotton. Many beings, *ONE* Ultimate Reality.

If you are wearing a gold necklace do I say "Please remove the necklace so I may see the gold"? I can't see the gold without seeing the necklace, and I can't see the necklace without seeing the gold.

There are multitudes of gold jewelry in the world, but there is only one substance "Gold." All the gold jewelry comes from this one substance, the jewelry takes many forms and shapes, but they all arise out of this *one* substance—*gold*.

The physical world isn't illusion or bad or fallen or *maya*—it is woven on the loom of the Gods out of Spirit Itself!

So the universe is *ONE*. The physical world is not separate from the spirit world. The physical world is like a exquisite Persian Carpet, and Spirit is like the threads that make up the carpet. Spirit then is the *ground of our being*.

Existence is not derived as such in the limited sense of being the creation of some "god", it is the *entity itself*. The observer is one and the mirrors are many.

The multiplicity of the mirrors does not affect the oneness of reflection in the numerous mirrors.

So we see then what a tenuous thing this physical world is. From this understanding we can draw certain conclusions about how best to cause changes in our physical world...in other words—how to make MAGICK! As the Neo-Pagan chant goes: "We are the weavers, we are the web."

IT

"It" doesn't care whether you go to church or not. "It" doesn't care whether you join a religion or not. "It" is a mystery that comes and goes as "It" wishes, and when "it" wishes. That is all there is to "It".

There is great danger in saying that "It" has to do with religion. There is great hazard in assuming one knows what "It" is. The more you try to identify "It" the more one confuses the issue. Beware of those who say they've bottled "It" and sell 'so-called' "It". "It" is not for sale.

"It" doesn't require that you change your behavior, although "It" may change you."

THE ROSWELL DECLARATION

Many people are greatly perturbed that the government of the United States hasn't released all the information it has in its files concerning UFO's. These individuals are seeking to introduce a law they call "The Roswell Declaration" which will declassify any information regarding UFO's or extraterrestrial intelligence. I agree that this information, if it does exist, is not something to which a privileged few in the United States government should have exclusive rights. It would be knowledge of profound importance to which all people throughout the world have an inalienable right.

In an Action/Adventure movie, the hero often finds him/herself being chased by some "bad guy" through a ware-house or some such labyrinthine place. The hero plays a game of cat and mouse, choosing various hiding places. In order to distract the "bad guy's" attention, the hero throws a pebble so that it hits in a different location than where the hero is situated. The 'bad' guy immediately starts firing his gun at where the pebble landed, and the hero skirts away quickly while the "bad guy" is thus distracted.

The mystery concerning UFO's is indeed worthy of investigation, yet it might be valuable to consider if the UFO controversy is a 'red-herring' that the government has created to distract our attention from other unidentified and unexplainable phenomena that are taking place. All our attention is being distracted onto UFO's; of what doesn't the government want us to become aware? What if there was really much more to this phenomena than saucers and ET's?

Some believe that the transformation of culture which dawned during the 1960's was watered down by a sudden introduction of a myriad of 'causes'—Ecology, Save-the-Whales, Anti-Nukes, Neo-Paganism, and so forth. I am not saying that we should ignore the extraterrestrial alien question. We should not discount that the government is diverting our energies and attention so we don't notice the something else which may be so monumental it currently escapes our notice.

If individuals wish more information on "The Roswell Declaration" they should write: Center for UFO Studies, 2457 W. Peterson Avenue, Chicago, IL 60659 and ask for a copy of the declaration.

We are so intent on having information released about what went on in the 1940's and 1950's regarding uniden-tified flying objects, that we are distracted from asking ourselves what classified top-secret governmental 'studies' and 'research' is going on *NOW*!

After signing the declaration ask yourself if you have heard of anything (besides UFO's) that is unusual and mysterious that would benefit from being examined. Are there energies out there that we are ignoring because our attention has been distracted by the UFO controversy? Powers, Non-Human Earth Intelligences, Forces, Time Travel, and Parallel Universes exist and we need to become aware of them. Soon as we limit our universe, and yes, concentrating on extraterrestrials and alien craft can divert us from other realities going on around us, we block from perception any possibilities existing outside our model of the universe.

In our quest to find Extraterrestrials, perhaps we are being deluded into not looking for Earthlings. Might a new organism be evolving on the Earth? A new way of looking at real occurrences is being cultivated by certain artists, writers, and thinkers. The dead weight of materialism has long since proven ineffective in explaining *BEING*. Perhaps there lurks on Earth *new* beings, and they are us! The powers that be might not want us to look at the most obvious of places: ourselves.

The new enigmas we find may be terrifying. Who says that the laws of the universe (in the way that we understand them) can not mysteriously evolve? The world was very different 5,000 years ago. Maybe the world will once again take another shift and people of the future will find us just as strange as we find the people of ancient Egypt. Maybe we will have Gods and Goddesses who walk the Earth with us. Maybe Angels will be common place and no one will be called crazy if they talk to dead relatives.

The world was once mythological. Then it became commonsensical as the magick evaporated into the books of science and academics. The rationalists then laughed at the minstrels who sang of a different world. Yet recently, academia has found that its delineations and borders are being deluged with new wonders. Are we at the end of an historical era?

Science long ago discovered that the Earth had shifted on its axis and sort of flopped over on its side in the ancient past. Many people know that the Sahara desert once flowed with water and the Arctic once bloomed with tropical plants. And once upon a time the Sun was a God and the Moon a Goddess. Rivers were great serpent-beings. Fairy folk and mortals regularly had contact, sometimes they even intermarried.

So how can anyone be sure that what we call "reality" is in fact a *fait accompli*? Mythology was reality to the people living it. Mythology is not a view of the world made up by primitive, young humanity and plastered over reality, but in fact was the way the world manifested to them! We may tend to forget that it wasn't too long ago, a mere couple of hundred of years, when our ancestors had daily experiences with the fairy world. Fairies helped with the farming, helped with the milking, helped protect the home.

What I am suggesting is that we try not to get too wrapped up in comfortable patterns. Every time we say "I am a _____", we chip away a little of our freedom. Baptists, Plumbers, Taoists, Democrats, Runners,

Teachers, Notary Publics and Philosophers, are all labels which instantly numb our senses. These senses could perceive a larger view of who we are!

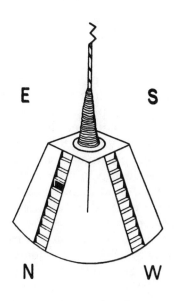

LIBERATION FROM BELIEF

When we give up our 'security blankets,' we free up an enormous amount of psychic energy. Oftentimes, when this energy is released it spontaneously creates magick in one's life. For instance, many people are so afraid of facing the *UNKNOWN* that they cling to a various paradigms: a given religion, philosophy, psychology, or political party. When these people decide to take a naked look at their beliefs, suddenly the enormous amount of energy expended in shoring up the paradigm is liberated to manifest one's desires.

Folks feel the need for continuity in their lives. Hence, the desire to follow a news story, a television series, soap operas, sports teams and so forth. Without continuity we feel surrounded by chaos. Yet, as magickians we know that chaos is the raw stuff of magick! I recommend that magickians stay aware of any patterns, habits, and routines into which they may be settling. Take a different route to work, listen to a different style of music, try out a fresh style of dress, comb your hair in a different style.

DO AFFIRMATIONS REALLY WORK?

When people try to use "faith" and "belief" as a method of creating change, they often end up only affirming their incapacity.

Take for example someone who wants to be empathic. Merely having faith and believing that one is empathic, does not make one empathic, even if the person keeps up the pretense to the end of his or her life.

When you say "I wish", you are affirming that you lack something. When you say "I can", you are telling yourself that you're incapable. Wishing lacks courage. It's a passive thing. It's based on a belief that you can't give it to yourself. We need to make a paradigm shift from wishing to *giving* to ourselves.

Inherent in "belief" exists a dishonesty of sorts. The Self knows this dishonesty, this hypocrisy. This kind of affirmation is, in truth, the *Affirmation of Inadequacy*. Robert Bly calls affirmations "optimistic lies." By bombarding the Self endlessly with affirmations, one is merely reminding oneself over and over that one is deficient in some way.

The true belief that hides behind the affirmation "I am empathic" is that one is incapable of empathy. *This True Belief Abides Organically In The Subconscious*. The belief is alive! It has an organic existence.

To believe (in a superficial way through affirmation) is but a show of pretense, and only serves to reinforce the qualities you are seeking to change. It does nothing to change the biotic pattern.

We are dealing only with the surface of our multi-leveled beings when we try to change our lives in this way. No wonder we can't cure cancer. If we are trying to affirm at a level that isn't even organic!

When we do affirm in the old way we cause the sub-conscious to react violently. For it is angered, irritated, and upset by the constant barrage of lies being told by the con-scious mind. It, in a word, reacts. And this reaction may take the form of an even greater outer materialization of just the opposite of what one wants to manifest—in this instance one could become so un-empathic that one in fact appears to others as cold and supercilious.

The organic belief is that one is incapable. When acted on by affirmations that state one is capable, the subconscious rebels by reinforcing and preserving the organic state. It digs its feet in even more, and becomes entrenched. Therefore, to change your life, I recommend that you make your belief organic *and* sub-conscious.

In *The Way of Power* we not only work on the subcon-scious level, but we go further and actually work on the organic or physical level of our beings.

One way to make your affirmations efficacious is to *sing* them! By turning your affirmations into song you are directly energizing them and simultaneously enlivening them on the subtle planes of existence. The process is something like incense smoke rising from the fiery coals up to the Gods. When you sing, chant, or intone, you *Inflame* yourself in Spirit. You light yourself on fire! In the act of singing the singer instantly goes into a state of trance and transcends the conscious. Through this transcendence the magickian directly changes the state of life conditions.

Many self-help tapes have affirmations on side A and subliminals on side B. The subliminal sides of your self-help tapes are so much more valuable than the affirmation side of those tapes. There is almost a Zen-like beauty to listening to messages that aren't heard. I am not implying that subliminal tapes do not function as their makers say they do, I think the jury is still out in that respect. These "subliminal" messages may or may not be heard by the subconscious mind. But it really doesn't matter. I find that they effectively demonstrate *The Way of Power*.

In listening to a subliminal tape, a person listens to "nothing" to achieve "something." When a person plays a subliminal tape there exists in that person's being an *Intention*. That intention is then projected into the *Great Silence* of the unheard subliminals. The subliminals are in a sense words from the Realm of No-Thought, in that they aren't heard by the conscious mind. From this realm of Voidness springs all manifestation.

One doesn't consciously hear any commands. There is no pressure brought to bear on the conscious mind. If the tapes *don't* work as the manufacturers say they do (delivering messages to the subconscious), this is even better, because then there is no pressure put on the subconscious.

The act of listening to a subliminal tape is like dropping a coin into a fountain. Your wish is your coin and the Realm of No-Thought, the fountain.

When businesses use subliminals to broadcast "I am honest. I do not steal. I pay for my purchases." masked by "Musak" over the public address system, then we are witnessing pure magick. I believe that it is not the "subliminal" effect that is so useful, but rather the *intention* of the manager of the store who is broadcasting these messages. This "intention" creates a magickal field within the store.

THE DEEPEST STRATUM

Beliefs have a life of their own. They exist physically in the neural pathways of the sub-conscious mind; they simultaneously exist metaphysically in the spirit realms.

If we follow the pathway down into the subconscious, we will eventually enter into the supersensible spirit realm.

Authorities in Jungian psychology state that the subconscious is the doorway to the "collective unconscious."

The "collective unconscious" can be defined as the inborn, unconscious, psychic material common to humankind, accumulated by the experience of all preceding generations. The collective unconscious is the *Akashic Record* written about and spoken of by sages and psychics for millennia.

Paradoxically, by journeying deeply into yourself, you are actually traveling further outside the mundane, day-to-day self! The further you travel into the stratum of experiences contained in your subconscious, the closer you get to truly powerful archetypal forces of the universe, until you eventually arrive at the Ultimate Reality itself!

ATAVISMS AND UFO'S

If we continue to journey further within ourselves, we uncover the past lives we lived as earlier evolutionary forms: animal, reptile, fish, protoplasm, and the rest! And if we continue our journey back into our unconscious we will discover our alien and inter-stellar origins.

Everything that has ever existed or will exist is contained here in these subconscious and organic realms.

Within our very cells we carry genetic memories of ancestral incarnations. If we awaken these atavisms to conscious life, we can take on their attributes and qualities. These atavistic powers have been known for millennia as: animal totems, helping spirits, maybe even the Gods and Goddesses themselves!

How would you like the force of a Tyrannosaurs Rex when you must ask your boss for a raise? This is the kind of power we manifest in *The Way of Power* when we contact the deepest recesses of our beings.

We do not simply skim the surface of our minds by repeating affirmation sentences all day long. With *The Way of Power* we actually awaken long dormant energies within the self that embody and personify the qualities and/or experiences that we wish to bring forth in our lives. We awake the *Sleeping Giant*!

I tend to believe that the amount of attention being focused on the subject of UFO's and aliens signifies humanity's growing awareness that God is *ALIEN*! He is no longer the Kindly Father who answers our prayers and forgives our sins.

After World War II many people began saying that God was Dead, that no Loving God could have permitted the extermination of 6 Million Jewish People. But now with the advent of the counter-culture and the New-Age Conscious-ness, people's spirituality is reawakening, but to a *very different kind of God!*

We are realizing the true WEIRDNESS and STRANGE-NESS of EXISTENCE. And if all this springs form some central source or point, that POINT must be very foreign, outlandish, exotic, in other words: ALIEN to us.

THE ASPECTS OF A HUMAN BEING

(Working from the level of immediate waking consciousness inward, the following states and experiences will be found inside the human being).

1. *Conscious Mind* (The Sentient or Aware Mind, which contains all that one is immediately cognizant of, and all memory which is accessible)

2. *Subconscious Mind* (The Storehouse of Memories)

Past Experiences (including the information that has come in through our senses which we didn't allow to become fully conscious—consider for example how people can remember license plate numbers when hypnotized.)

Past Human Lives (it may be helpful to remember that humanity is exceedingly old. Most people will go back in the past-life regressions only a few hundred or thousand years, not pausing to consider that humanity has existed for *millions* of years on this earth. Therefore, in all that time each of us has mastered innumerable skills, faculties, and talents, and these abilities are all alive and present in the subconscious waiting to be tapped.

We have recorded and stored thousands of years of experiential information).

Pre-Human Past Lives: Animal, Bird, Fish, Plant, Mineral Incarnations (we have all experienced pre-human lifetimes as we made the journey from the Primeval Oceans to our Ape-like ancestors).

Future Lives (we can access interdimensionally our far-future lives. *We* are the Ancestors of our Future Selves! Our future selves are at this very moment looking back into their past and trying to make contact with us. They can "time-warp" into the present).

Post- and Pre-Human Selves and Extra-Terrestrial Alien Incarnations (we are connected both through our distant *past* AND through our distant *future* with SELVES that are inter-galactic. Our origin and ultimate destiny lies in the stars).

Antecedents of the Human Race (The Deep Ones. Severe and forbidding guardians of the Gate through which the Outer Forces ever seek to enter human space and time).

Outside Human Space and Time (The Great Ones of the Outer Void. "People who come for the other side of the sea" of interstellar space).

The Void (The Unmanifest, The Noumenon, Chaos, through which all continually flows into existence. Everything which exists (all manifestation, all phenomena) streams out of the Void into existence).

ANGER

Anger is just one pole of the magnet. It is not superior or inferior to any other emotion. We need to embrace our anger.

By that I mean, we want to recognize the sacredness of anger. Many deities from all around the world depict "anger" in a sacred way. Kali, The Morrigan, Hades, Set, Mars, Minerva, Lugh, Thor, Vulcan, Odin, and Fion Mac Cumhail are all deities that express a divine kind of anger.

They are the avengers, hunters, protectors, and warriors; Gods and Goddesses of death and slaughter. Even the Christian God Jesus took a whip and beat the money-changers in the temple in Jerusalem and cursed a fig-tree for not bearing fruit!

Anger is a part of the divine interplay of the universe. It is part of the Cosmic Dance.

Instead of condemning yourself for feeling anger, recognize that your anger is a sacred, integral aspect of ALL THAT IS.

There is nothing wrong with emotion; it is when we *act* on our emotions that we must then be prepared to accept the consequences of our actions. This is not to put a value-judgment on actions or on consequences...but it is a wake-up call to be careful to analyze ALL the consequences of one's actions...be they legal, karmic, emotional, mental, or physical consequences.

LEARN HOW TO
CLEAR THE MIND

Often it is through a process of emptying the mind that transformation can occur. Ironically, the most powerful changes in our life can be triggered by a moment of emptiness.

What is this "moment of emptiness"? It is the time when the mind has been quieted for one reason or another. Often it is the moment when a person has completely exhausted all his or her options and completely gives up all the mind's schemes, plans, and stratagems.

The 12-Step Program concept of "Let Go and Let God" is applicable here; this is one reason why "The Program" has been so helpful to so many people. For it is often only when one has "hit bottom" that one can truly empty oneself, dump the garbage, clean the slate, erase the disk, and begin anew!

There are other ways to create this "moment of emptiness" besides having to "hit bottom." One method would be to perform physical exercise till a state of exhaustion is achieved.

Another technique is through sexual stimulation to the point of orgasm, when the mind suddenly goes blank, and we experience what the French call the *petit mort*, or little death.

ANSWER YOUR OWN PRAYER

From time immemorial people have prayed to their Creator. Many of you reading this book have probably resorted to prayer on occasion to petition certain favors from the Divine Source. But I invite you to now look at prayer from a unique perspective.

One of the missions of the "New Age" was to help us all to become more aware of our inherent divinity. The "New Age" taught the general public that each person is an embodiment of the Divine. However, individuals on the path of Magick and the Western Mystery Tradition often think that prayer is beneath them, a kind of inferior way of working. Permit me to suggest another way of looking at prayer.

Let us apply the "New Age" revelation of inherent divinity to our new way of looking at prayer. You may begin by saying your prayer in whatever form or manner you choose. After saying your prayer to whatever deity you are praying to, I suggest you then visualize yourself *AS* that very God/dess looking down on you! This is called assuming a "God-form."

In ancient cultures, such as the Celtic and the Sumerian, individuals experienced the Gods moving through them. An architect would say: "The gods build the great cities."

Let's take it step-by-step: you begin by saying a prayer in your own words, to whatever Higher Power to which you pray. Then visualize yourself *as* that particular God, Goddess, Archangel, Super-Hero, Fairy, Mythological Being, Tree, or Deva to whom you just prayed. Feel that

YOU are your Higher Power! Actually take on the form (in your mind) of your Ultimate Source.

As that Divine Being say some words to this effect: "Yes, (insert your name), I hear your prayer, and will grant you your wish as you desire. I love you and hear and answer you." Then shower forth love onto yourself and see yourself having what you asked for, *but from the perspective of God/dess looking upon you*.

Now you have completed the cycle full circle! You acknowledge that you are both the one praying and the one being prayed to. Your prayer can't help but be answered under these circumstances.

ARCHETYPES

Everything in the universe has a support or energy by which it is upheld. This support or energy is known as an archetype.

How do you recognize a chair? There are millions of different chairs in the world, yet you recognize a chair as being a chair in a fraction of a second! How is that? There must be some concept in your mind of what a chair looks like, a kind of perfect chair. From this concept of "chair" you deduce that the object in front of you is in fact a chair and you can sit down on it. This concept of "chair" is one kind of archetype that exists on the mental plane.

An archetype then is a pattern, model, or paradigm of a given thing. We contain in our minds archetypes for thousands of things. But as we know, whatever exists on the mental plane also exists on the spiritual plane. In the spirit realms, there dwell archetypes of objects and possessions such as: chair, bridge, road, house, car, etc., as well as archetypes for qualities and powers such as: courage, beauty, grace, passion, love, strength, and so on.

BLUEPRINTS

Whenever one wishes to build anything on the physical plane a blueprint is required. We can see this principle demonstrated every day in the world around us. Every bridge, building, highway, boat, car, and so forth, first existed as a plan in someone's mind.

Only then, after the conception was well thought out, was the plan drawn-up as a blueprint on the designer's or architect's drafting table.

After these first two stages, the actual physical materialization of the plan goes into effect. So we perceive three distinct stages:

1. *conception.*
2. *plan.*
3. *physical action.*

To sum up: an archetype is the subtle cause for the physical manifestation of anything in this universe.

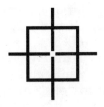

MAKE ROOM FOR WHAT YOU WANT

You do not need to wrestle what you want away from someone else. There's no need to be jealous and competitive in this life. All you have to do is to tune-in to the archetype of your desired goal.

Once you're tuned-in, then I recommend you provide a pathway for this archetype to manifest on the physical plane. For instance, if you want a car, but don't have a garage or parking space, you are blocking the flow of the car to you. Or if you want a wife but live in a rooming house with ten other guys, then there is no space for her to fit into your life.

Please read between the lines here. You've got to make room in your life for what you want. You need to create channels for your desired goal to flow to you, and to do that you need to make space in your regular routine, in your home, in your car (clean out that clutter on the front seat), and in the way you think.

If you keep thinking your usual thoughts and doing your usual habitual actions, then the NEW and DIFFERENT cannot enter into your LIFE!

Smell new scents (try a different cologne...maybe stop wearing cologne for a while and just smell the natural "you"...try switching to "oils" instead of colognes), see new sights, take new and different roads to work, try out new foods and restaurants (eat a piece of fruit you've never eaten before, order a dish at the Chinese take-out that you've never tried), start to interrupt the meta-psychic programming of your mind. You need to shake yourself up—unsettle the mind! Break the old patterns. Open a window in your life and let in some *Fresh Air*! Wake up those tired old mind-paths and blaze some new neural pathways in your brain.

This will disrupt the old energy-fields that you have in your brain and will in turn change the energy-field in the environment around you.

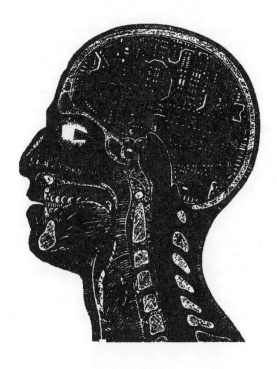

I'M SO EXCITED!

Raise your excitement level! *Start vibrating at the frequency of that which you want!!!*

To do this you must get so close to your goal that you can practically taste it! If you want to manifest a car, go to show-rooms and test drive new cars. Get brochures. Read car magazines. Cut out pictures of the cars you'd like to have and stick them up on your walls . Maybe buy some fuzzy-dice, a can of fresh car scent. The sense of smell is very ancient and certain odors can awaken deep impulses and memories inside ourselves. Fill your senses, in a real way, with your goal and this will trigger your subconscious into action!

I suggest that you go beyond just picturing your goals. To the extent that it is possible, I want you to actually experience your goals physically. Engage ALL your senses.

Now of course not everything can be experienced for various reasons, and I don't recommend breaking the law. However, just about any goal can be experienced at least partially in some physical sense.

If you want to go on a dream vacation, rent some travelogues from your local video store, go to travel agents and pick up brochures, hang posters of the place you want to visit on your walls.

THE UNMISTAKABLE STAMP

Don't worry, I'm not going to tell you what thousands of other visualization practitioners have taught, that you must be clear about your intentions. You know that already.

But you can't stop there. To make your magick effective, I recommend that you taste and smell your goal in a very precise and specific way. Then your whole being becomes magnetized and naturally reaches out, embraces, and accepts that goal into your life.

The trick is to think of something UNIQUE about what you want. This somehow bypasses the brains usual defenses against being harassed by "visualizations." So if you want a car, think of your ideal car, but picture the exact kind of tachometer, upholstery, or engine that you want.

If you want a lover, picture his/her body EXACTLY the way you would like it to be, and then concentrate on one part of it as you visualize. You have to teach your mind to FOCUS. Unless the mind is focused it will tend to dissipate the built-up magickal tension. You don't want ALL cars, lovers, apartments, and so on, you want one, so BE SPECIFIC!

You may not get exactly what you visualized for, but what you receive *will* have the unmistakable stamp of your visualization, and you will recognize it when it appears.

BINDING THE OPPOSING FORCE

In the past, magickians have sought to bind the opposing force of the force they invoke. With *The Way of Power*, however, this is not necessary, for when you utilize *The Triangle of Manifestation* you firmly secure the archetype of your desire at the point from which everything visible and invisible arises.

Because the wish has been equilibrated and burned in the purifying fires of the "Triangle of Manifestation", the materialization is inherently balanced against the swing of the pendulum.

THE EQUILATERAL
CROSS

An added symbol of the secret workings of manifestation is the equilateral cross. The Center Point of the cross is exactly equidistant from each of the arms. All sides are equal.

Meditate upon this image, focusing your mind upon the Center Point. Try to imagine the point at which all four directions meet. This is the secret 'heart of hearts' of the Equilateral Cross. Allow all other distractions to fade into the distance as you allow yourself to follow the center deeper and deeper into the Point of Equilibrium.

FIX YOUR HEART TO A STAR

Inflame your mind with your heart's desire; then start taking pragmatic action on the material plane to trigger the manifestation of your desire.

Don't worry about failure. Individual instances of failure don't matter! The secret to bringing your goals forward into sight is to detach your mind and emotions from results. Pretend that you are a scientist doing a series of experiments. A scientist expects to fail quite a number of times before s/he gets it right. You are focused on your desire! The divine archetype is emanating an irresistible force that will see to it that your dream comes true, just keep the image of your goal ahead of you, and like a sea-captain looking at the Pole-Star, continue moving towards it.

Before a sailor sets sail in the morning, s/he checks the wind direction. The sailor may have a preference as to the direction of the wind, but nevertheless, he or she will trim the sails accordingly. Sailors do not say: "Because the wind blows from the west today, we won't sail." Use unpleasant experiences as valuable *feed-back* which will enable you to more exactly chart your course.

Just because the wind is not blowing in the direction you want is not a reason to give up! Trim your sails according to the direction of the wind, and you still can keep moving in the heading that you want.

Quantum Physics teaches us that subatomic particles (the vanguards of matter) don't *exist* until someone pays attention to them. Before attention, they are waves in the field of infinite possibilities. Your focused attention will draw the possibility *you* want out of the *Sphere of Infinite Possibilities*. The more clearly you define what you want, the more you will obtain what you want. To the degree that you concentrate your attention onto "how bad it is out there", or "there really are no openings for me in my field", or "see how [mean/cruel/dangerous/crazy/heart-less/rejecting] they are," to that degree you will elicit out of the field of infinite possibilities a reality that matches exactly what you concentrate upon.

MAGNETIZE YOURSELF FOR SUCCESS

Have you ever known people who walk around with a cloud over their head? Their car might break down one day, the next day their hamster dies, followed quickly by their television set being repossessed and their boss firing them.

These people seem to be subject to an unrelenting series of outrageous acts of fate. We all have met these people and sometimes it seems that they are us!

Why is this so? Are the people who walk into psychiatrist's offices and say, "It seems that the universe is out to get me": crazy?

No, they're not. What happens is that the person has become *magnetized for unhappiness*. There are two worlds, two whirlwinds of energy if you will, that co-exist simultaneously. You can call them Parallel Universes or Energy Vortices of Circumstance.

When we are sad and upset and believe that things are against us, we are *attuning* our minds to a certain *frequency*. That frequency then tends to invite in similar circumstances to support and reinforce the main frequency. These circumstances are real, as far as "real" goes, to the person involved! The universe *is* really out to get the paranoid person!!!

We all know the saying "When it rains it pours." This expresses the same idea stated above that similar frequencies tend to support and reinforce each other. Another famous adage expressing the theory of mental attunement is: "Things always happen in three's." When you develop

a certain mind-set, you are actually *entering into that world!*
You are stepping into a particular reality-tunnel.

The best way to exit such a *negative* tunnel is not through
some grand scheme or Ten-Year Ritual, but to repeatedly
do *one small task!* Think of little Bilbo Baggins or Frodo
from "The Lord of the Rings" by J.R.R. Tolkien. Both were
"Hobbits", the smallest, most insignificant creature in
Middle-Earth. But because they were so "unimportant" in
the eyes of certain great and powerful beings around at
that time, they were able to sneak into the enemy's realm
and confound him!!!

I recommend that you devise one small task, that you
can repeat *ad infinitum* all day. For instance, if you want to
have more friends, you may not need a complete course in
"How to Win Friends and Influence People" by Dale
Carnegie. Try the small task of saying hello and smiling at
as many strangers as you can. This one small effort can
undermine an entire *energy vortex* of Negativity!

Or you could hum or sing a tune. The frequency of your
song will undermine the frequency of your sorry set of
circumstances and completely break the unwanted reality-
tunnel into pieces.

THE FLOW OF TIME

Here is a big occult secret: *Time flows in both directions at once*! In other words, we are not only being carried along into the future on an ocean wave of time, but the future is at this very moment flowing towards us! The point where we meet head-on is called the present.

The wise ones know that we have some degree of control as to what future flows to us. We can select an ideal future out of an array of possible futures.

One technique of *The Way of Power* is to imagine our future as we want it to be and then visualize it slowly flowing to us from out of the future. To help you in doing this you can choose to think of time as a flowing river.

Notice how the current carries the water down river. In your mind's eye, see your desired future upriver. See it being carried along on the current. Feel it reaching out to you and flowing towards you like the river flows towards you. Say to yourself: "My heart's desire is coming in my direction!"

Next step is to visualize going out and meeting our future. Actually see yourself in your present day-to-day surroundings and then find a way to connect up with the future you are visualizing flowing to you from the future.

For example, visualize your soul-mate. Now put your soul-mate on the same side-walk you stroll every day to work. See her/him walking towards you. See yourselves meeting. This is what I mean by connecting the present up to the future you desire. We behold our present and future meeting! It is very important while doing this visualization to note *how* your future goals arrive. Information can be pre-cognitively revealed to you while doing this exercise so observe any unusual or unexpected details you encounter in the visualization.

If you are visualizing for the perfect mate and you suddenly see the two of you meeting on the beach...it might be in your best interest to see if you can identify the particular beach, and then, in real life, go and frequent it!

YOU ALREADY HAVE WHAT YOU WANT

You already have what you want! The fulfillment of what you desire is hidden in the fact of your not having it at this present time. *Everything contains hidden within it, its exact polar opposite*. Within a lonely heart lies the seed of love's fulfillment.

What you are doing through *The Way of Power* is the great Work of all esoteric masters, that is, to make the unconscious conscious. You are peering behind the veil and acknowledging the hidden side of reality. You recognize that for every night there is a day, or for every winter, a summer. Let the rhythms of nature be your encouragement and help you to know that the future can be different.

With *The Way of Power* on your side you do not need to stand there helplessly and watch the pendulum swing back and forth. Through use of *The Triangle of Manifestation* and the other techniques outlined here, you can *equilibrate* your wishes and thereby stabilize them on the material plane.

RESPECTING OUR INNER SELVES

This kind of magical work accomplishes something else. It shows respect for yourself. It is superior to "affirmations" in that you are not ramming down your throat clichéd, trite, stale concepts that you feel phony about stating.

I believe rather than trying to wear a cheerful mask until it fuses to your face, you should rather magickally endeavor to *remove* all masks (at least to yourself) and discover what lies *behind the mask*. The goal is to remove the facade and acknowledge the various emotions that make up the real you. It has been said that emotions are the thoughts of God. Honor and respect them—even the scary, angry, hateful feelings.

Each time you balance a thought with its inherent contradiction, you are recognizing the many layers of your personality. You thereby give respect to those parts of yourself (in your subconscious) that for whatever reason do not want you to have what you consciously want. You are allowing that subconscious part of you to speak up, be understood, and be acknowledged.

When we don't give voice to that part of ourselves, we are inviting all sorts of trouble into our lives. For that part of us speaks whether we invite it to or not. But it speaks in its own way. Maybe we develop an ulcer, a facial tick, perhaps we get depressed, or can't concentrate on the work at hand. Those trapped thought-forms need to see the light of day...they need to express themselves! *The Way of Power* respects *all* the aspects of our being.

I put so much emphasis on the integration of the individual magickian and his or her neural programming for the reason that effective magick is not so much based on what you *know*, but on what you *are*!

WISDOM FROM THE QABALAH

Let's take a look at some of the theory behind *The Way of Power.* To do so, we will draw from concepts taught in the Hebrew Qabalah.

The Qabalah forms the basis of the Western Mystery Tradition. It is a system of mystical knowledge and spiritual development in the same way that Yoga is the mystical system of the East.

Central to Qabalistic teachings is the concept of the "Tree of Life." This "tree" is a diagram of the entire cosmos, and the soul of man as related thereto; this diagram includes the aspects of: Cause, Force, Receptivity, Preservation, Destruction, Equilibrium, Nature, Mind, Emotion, and Physicality.

It is a cosmic diagram; the blueprint of the universe and the human being, containing within itself a description of all possible relationships and all phenomena.

What's important to grasp from an initial exposure to the "Tree of Life" is that as one ascends the tree, going from the earth plane into the various spiritual planes, duality disappears! From the perspective of someone at the top of the tree, destruction and creation are both manifestations of the One. We can say that at the top of the tree there exists the Ultimate Reality that transcends all other realities.

In human physiology we can find a clear illustration of this concept of Ultimate Reality. Metabolism consists of anabolism, or the ingesting and assimilating of food, and catabolism, or the breaking down of tissue in order to create energy. In order for us to be alive (to be *one living being*) we need to have both forces at work in our bodies.

Our physical "ultimate reality" lies in the perfect balance of both forces.

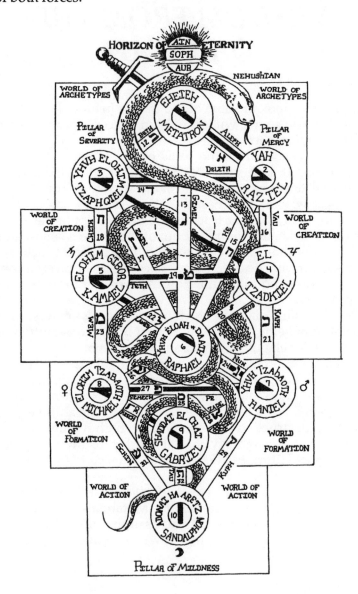

THE SECRET HEART
OF AUM

We see the master-plan of the universe in operation in the Hindu mantra "AUM." The spelling of the word is a clue to the art of magickal operation and perfectly portrays *The Triangle of Manifestation* .

It is taught by the yogis that by the letter "A" is meant the *protector* of the world. The letter "U" denotes the Being which *dissolves* it; "M" stands for its *creator*.

So in *The Way of Power* terminology, the letter "A" is the up-building force, the letter "U" the down-breaking force, and the letter "M" the apex of transcendence which reconciles the two.

AN ANALOGY TAKEN FROM UNIVERSITY LIFE

Realism must balance idealism. Consider a university campus, for example. On the one hand, we have idealistic students who are willing to challenge any idea, take on the authorities, conceive of and try out new approaches, and remove whatever has outlived its usefulness.

The students can be relentless in their drive to eliminate unfair grading practices, sexism, harassment, incompetent professors, and administrators that are hopelessly behind the times. They tear down (catabolism) the old and out-dated aspects of the institution to make way for a new and more enlightened system. Change is responsible for all of evolution.

On the other hand, we have the administration which represents the opposing force.

The administration wants to keep things as they have always been. Their energy seeks to preserve and protect the traditional order of the university. The administration stands for that which is secure, stable, and steady. They are the establishment.

The administration builds up (anabolism) the university by: the construction of new buildings and fund raising activities which assure that the university will continue on into the future.

Hence, realism must balance idealism. Each force checks the other, if not the ensconced administration would lead the school into stagnation and the student force if unchecked, would lead the school into chaos.

(Of course this analogy is only for the purposes of illustration; in actuality, there are many professors who are on the cutting edge of innovation and many students who have completely bought into the system).

Therefore, any idea that contains within itself both the positive and the negative, the active and the latent, and the male and the female, partakes of the very nature of the Ultimate Reality. When you participate in the very nature of the Ultimate Reality you become imbued with the power to bring forth your goals into existence.

This concept of the integrating of opposites is the very heart of *The Way of Power* .

HINDU PHILOSOPHY

Let us consider the Hindu trinity of: Brahma, Siva, and Vishnu in light of *The Way of Power* .

In Hindu philosophy we see echoes of the same principal at work. Brahma is the embodiment of the quality of passion, or desire, by which the world was called into being. Siva, is the embodiment of the destructive fire by which the world is consumed; *Vishnu* is the embodiment of the property of mercy and goodness by which the world is preserved.

In the Hindu pantheon of Brahma, Siva, and Vishnu, we have an illustration of the three points of *The Triangle of Manifestation*. Vishnu is the sustaining force which brings us what we want; Siva, the breakdown force, which is the destruction inherent in the desire; and Brahma the Third Point of Transcendence, The Point of Infinite Possibility, The Point of Creation, which balances both forces.

THE TRIANGLE OF MANIFESTATION AS ENCOUNTERED IN THE TAROT

The Tarot is filled with images of the balance and harmony of opposing forces.

The High Priestess sits between two pillars named Jachin and Boaz. These two pillars stood before the Temple of Solomon. They represent the Light and the Dark. The Black Pillar of Boaz represents the negative life force (the down-breaking force) and the White Pillar of Jachin, the positive life force (the up-building force). Her mysterious presence IS the mystery of the Union of Opposites. She is the Middle Pillar.

The Chariot card depicts a chariot being drawn by two sphinxes. The two sphinxes represent the two hemispheres of the human brain: the right and left brains. In the two hemispheres of the brain we see the bottom two points of *The Triangle Of Manifestation*.

But as human beings we are not split down the middle in regards to our minds for we unite the two minds into *one consciousness*. This holistic integration of the two hemispheres of the brain is the Third Point of Transcendence, and is represented by the Charioteer in *The Chariot* tarot card.

In *Strength* we see a woman opening or closing the mouth of a lion. We don't know exactly which action she is executing. The lion represents the physical world and our physical bodies. The Woman is in a state of *BALANCE* in regard to the lion: poised at the very point of "neither-neither" in which all things are possible.

REVERBERATIONS OF THE FIRST ESSENCE

Life and spirit are created when two opposing forces combine synergistically; this is the essence of *The Way of Power*.

In other words, it is only when we balance a force with its inherent contradiction do we enable that force to become alive and incarnate on this planet!

The force that we invoke in *The Way of Power* IS the energy behind all manifestation. Another name for this energy is the *Ontos* or the Essence of essences. The Ontos is the essential nature of anything. Plotinus, a Roman philosopher born in Egypt in 205 C.E., *called this energy the First Hypostasis* (literally, to cause to stand). What stands? The erection (the Point). What causes the erection? The Triangle (The Source of Mystery—Woman—*that which causes to stand.*)

THE WAY OF POWER

We begin by attuning ourselves to the mind-set of the ALL. To accomplish this we need to go beyond the dualistic way of viewing the world and travel to the center of bliss.

First, resist the tendency towards dichotomized thinking. When you walk around saying to yourself: "I'm good; he's bad," or: "I'm cool; she's a jerk," or: "I'm normal; he's weird," your thinking is dichotomized or SPLIT.

When you view the world like this you are creating duality in your life. In this state, you are divided against yourself.

There is a hidden "occult" side to dichotomized thinking of which most people are ignorant. When we label someone a "jerk" the person we have labeled is actually making us feel uncomfortable about some part of ourselves that we feel is jerky; rather than admit this fact to ourselves, we *pretend* that he or she has the problem and not us.

This is a sure sign that subconsciously we are aware (or worried) that we have similar traits—perhaps certain traits that we secretly would like to give expression to, but are afraid to enact for various reasons.

So we have to return and embrace all our "Prodigal Sons and Daughters" inside ourselves. One advanced technique that can be used to achieve this integration of opposites is as follows: every now and then do the precise thing that bothers you so much in the behavior of other people. If you think people drive inconsiderately...drive inconsiderately; if you think people are dishonest, be dishonest; if you think people are phony, be phony. Now many people *rebel* at the thought of this. But when practiced *occasionally* this technique helps you to connect with the behavior you outwardly abhor and denounce...the behavior which actually secretly fascinates you. The technique will help you to integrate rejected aspects of yourself and consolidate your Will.

Or perhaps we are expressing these traits already but are *unaware* of our words and actions. We may be in a state of *denial*.

In order to go beyond thinking in terms of our goals, it is essential that we destroy any concept of having or not having. It is crucial to rise above any thoughts about whether we are wealthy or poor, failures or successes, talented or untalented, lonely or loved, happy or sad.

We want to transcend these concepts, finding a contentment within ourselves, not a contentment of being lazy, but a contentment which helps us to live in the now and to accept the moment without judging it.

If the word "contentment" bothers you, instead think of this process in terms of "acknowledgment." We want to acknowledge our existence by simply observing our life without passing judgment on it.

It is not so much depression which causes people to commit suicide, but the individual's reaction to his or her depression. Interestingly enough, suicidal impulses are often disguised inclinations of rage and anger towards others. This graphically represents how the inherent contradiction in every idea lies buried only waiting for us to uncover it. In the case of suicide, it's often when the individual faces the rage inside himself or herself that integration and healing can begin.

If we can learn to just *BE* with ourselves no matter what state we're in, without trying to change ourselves, we generate *true* self love. For through this *beingness* we are finally *listening* to ourselves rather than trying to change ourselves. Sometimes our heart doesn't need so much of a "self-help project" as it simply needs us to pay attention to what it is feeling at the moment. This is true power...the power of being one with yourself!

The instant we start to judge, we kill the moment, the magick fades, and possibilities start to narrow. When we are judgmental we enter the realm of duality, the realm of dichotomy. But when we simply acknowledge our situation, we raise ourselves to the point that exists beyond these catalogs of opposites. *That* is the point of MAGICK!

Again, I am not saying to do nothing about changing a bad situation. We must take action. We must put wheels on our prayers. But to live life in a constant state of dissatisfaction, not only gives you a painful life, but it keeps you from grasping the real power behind this universe.

CONTENTMENT

Some people fear that if they allow themselves to be content, they won't do anything. They think they will just sit on their duff and allow life to pass them by. This is an error.

Often these very same people are trying to find an excuse not to be happy. They are forever postponing happiness until a certain set of criteria are fulfilled; for example, they think they will be happy when they get a new car, get married, or win a million dollars.

Yet these things never bring happiness. Happiness is a choice you make. Don't punish yourself and condemn yourself to a life of sadness.

When a person ceases to be judgmental and allows him or herself to be content, the person then becomes aligned and in harmony with the universe and acts effectively and powerfully in accord with the purpose of the universe.

YOU GOT TO BE IN IT TO WIN IT

Yes, I'm suggesting a completely new way for you to view the world. We need to accept more (in the sense of non-judgmental acknowledgment) and complain less. Paradoxically, one way to create change is to *be* with the problem rather than trying to get around it or rid of it.

Another technique is to do exactly the opposite of what you perceive to be the wrong the world is doing to you. If you think people aren't friendly to you, go out of your way to be warm and friendly to them! Again, work with the concept of "BALANCE"; redress people's apparent coldness by *your* warmth.

I'm *not* saying to do this with any phony emotionality, but practice this exercise in a detached "experimental" frame of mind. You are practicing magick; do not try to be optimistic. Simply be friendly while continuing to be true to your emotions.

To really live your life, you need to be in it. To be in your life means to allow it to happen around you. It seems like a contradiction on the surface. But by ceasing trying to control people and events, we actually allow the real meaning of one's life to become apparent.

We stop trying to force our template of reality over reality and instead let reality speak for itself.

And how do we do this? By breathing. By centering. By letting the world speak to you, instead of constantly listening to the chatter that goes on inside your head.

The world does speak. And we must listen. We're so busy speaking to ourselves that we have forgotten that simply by quieting ourselves and letting the experience of the universe flow into our souls, we will gain such wisdom that it will astound us!

SOMETHING TO THINK ABOUT

Often people experience frustration in their attempts to render manifest their wishes through magick. This is because the bottom line is usually the issue of *wanting* or *not wanting* the stated goal.

Sometimes before work can begin on manifesting our goal, we must first work on whether or not we *really* want this goal to manifest.

HOW TO SUPER-CHARGE THE TRIANGLE OF MANIFESTATION

To Super-Charge *The Triangle of Manifestation* we begin by sitting down with our hands open on our lap, or by our sides.

Let's use the example of wanting to find a suitable love partner. We start by visualizing in the left hand various pictures of our having the love partner of our dreams, doing all we want with our love partner, traveling, getting married, raising a family, making love, and the rest. Accompanying these pictures should also be the corresponding emotions of great joy, contentment, sexual thrills, fulfillment, peace, and the overwhelming feeling that yes, indeed, "I am loved."

Then we sense our right hand and place into it as many instances that we can think of in which the correlative of love is in action. For instance, we might place into the palm of that hand images of a person exercising tough-love or a parent allowing a child to experience pain in order to learn a lesson. We could also imagine ourselves in a "secret" marriage or an "arranged" marriage—any example of the correlative of love in action can be used.

We also place into this palm of the right hand all the feeling that accompanies these scenes—our sense of sadness, yet at the same time an awareness that all this is necessary for real love to be expressed.

Bounce back and forth a few times from hand to hand until both hands are fully "charged" with these feeling-pictures. Begin phasing mentally with this continuum and then when you feel you have reached a peak of sensation, rapidly bring both hands together in a loud CLAP!

Suspend all thought! Go into the Silence. Be aware of the feeling that this union generates. Slowly bring your hands to your chest to your heart chakra, and let the experience sink deeply into your being.

SAVE YOUR MARRIAGE

Frequently marriages are 'on the rocks' because the concept of equilibration is unknown to the marital partners. Frankly, many people would be upset to hear my advice as it applies to marriage, and so would not even try out my suggestions. For that advice is this: no matter how much you love someone, over time a reservoir of animosity will automatically be built up within you. Not through any fault of your own, but because *any* time a person builds up a positive charge, simultaneously a negative charge will emerge.

Now many people don't want to face this fact. They want to *pretend* that they have no hostile feelings towards their beloved. This is the weakness of people who deny that they have a shadow. At times you may even feel hatred towards your beloved. Do not be afraid. The pendulum can swing back to center. In fact, by accepting and realizing that there is animosity present in the marriage, you have taken the first step to healing that animosity!

The primary factor to be considered is that, as much as love is important in a marriage, so too must that love be balanced by the contradictory force inherent in love in order for that marriage to work!

A couple should, as much as possible, participate in physical games and sports in which they have the opportunity to hit things (such as golf and tennis). The object being to allow aggression, hostility, and violence, out in a safe atmosphere.

To try to solve relationship difficulties by re-affirming love over and over again, completely leaves out the sea of

113

hostile emotion which must be addressed and allowed to diffuse. Pillow fights, Squirt-Gun battles, Croquette, and Badminton all give expression to the opposing force of that which we want to invoke, namely love. You can wield those spongy plastic bats that are used to slam your spouse. When you need to vent or take out your anger, you boff your husband as hard as you can. What these toys do is give you a chance to take a reflective look at yourself, which usually causes a laugh. There are foam rubber hammers that do the same trick. These sports act as the *equilibrant* in the relationship, restoring the relationship to balance.

PART III

USING THE
WAY OF POWER

BODY-BUILDING MAGICK

Let's now apply the principles of *The Way of Power* to Body-Building.

First you want to clearly picture yourself looking the way you desire, with your muscles developed to the extent you wish... BUT, make it clear to yourself that this is you in the future, not just anytime in the future but at a specific date.

You can do this by simply saying to yourself: "This is me in six months" (or whatever time frame you want). Or you could write down on paper something like this: "In six months I will have the body I want."

This will alert your subconscious to the fact that it has a specific time frame to work within. It will begin to take the necessary steps to bring your body to the degree of development that you have stipulated.

Or you can picture yourself looking precisely the way you want to look and reading a newspaper with the desired target date on it.

CONSTRUCTION SITE MAGICK

A powerful tool of *The Way of Power* is to time your weight-training with the erection of a new building. Pick out some large office building under construction near where you live or work. Go to the location and study it. There's usually a poster which depicts the finished product at the corner of the construction site. Study that picture too. And then when you go home you can picture yourself standing in front of the completed building with exactly the kind, cut, and definition of muscles that you want.

If you go to the building every day, the actual energy of the workers and the process of the building being erected will work inside you to build up your thought-forms. As you stand by the building say to yourself: "As the building rises up guided by the invisible force of the blueprint, so too is my goal being brought forth into light by invisible spirit forces. Behold a symbol of an idea made manifest."

You are connecting yourself in a deep sub-conscious manner with the erection of the building. As the building grows, so do your muscles. Your mind will be filled with the concept of growth and enlargement.

This process can of course be used with any goal that is in harmony with the concept of growth, for example: financial prosperity, building an extension on your house, increasing your clientele, working on a doctoral thesis, cultivating your garden, rising up through the ranks in your business or organization, and developing your magickal vitality.

PLANT MAGICK

An additional *Way of Power* technique can be accomplished with a plant. Plant a seed in a pot and watch it grow. Know that as the etheric nature forces guide the seed to grow and manifest as a beautiful plant, so too do spirit forces nurture the seed of your desire into reality.

MASTURBATION MAGICK

Do you want a lover? Do you need to be held and to make love? I recommend *Masturbation Magick*.

Through the act of masturbation you can bring forth a sexual/love partner. This is some of the most powerful magick on earth and can sometimes produce astonishing results within a matter of hours!

The way to truly *energize* masturbation magick is to mimic, as far as possible, the actual motions of sex and/or intercourse along with the full body spasms of orgasm.

You must get your spine and pelvis in motion! This triggers the primitive (unconscious) areas of your brain that are in direct contact with the ancient archetypal forces. The orgasm reflex directly stimulates the magickal centers of the brain. Notice I did not say "orgasm"; the entire body must discharge its built up sexual energy in clonic convulsions.

So move around, thrust, thrash about, and make noise like you were actually having sex with another human being!

Get your spine and your hips moving. Remember, it is there in the cradle of the hips that the Kundalini and Sexual Chakras reside. So get your body into motion to awaken *them* into motion! Take some dance classes!

As your pelvis and spine move in the waves of orgasmic reflex, your body tells the mind that you are *serious* about having sex with a real sex partner—*and not just fantasizing*!

An orgasm involves the entire body. If only your genitals move or get aroused, if you only feel pleasure from your crotch during orgasm, *then you are not experiencing a full orgasm*! And the secret to *Magick* is *Complete Involvement!*

MARRIAGE MINDED?

Likewise, if you want to get married here are some techniques which you can use: Buy wedding magazines. Go to weddings. Go to catering halls and watch brides and grooms entering for their receptions. Plan your honeymoon. Price bridal gowns or tuxedos. Try some on. Go with a platonic friend of the opposite sex and look at wedding and engagement rings and try them on. Rent as many romantic movies as you can.

Fill your consciousness to overflowing with romance, love, and marriage. And here is one thing to remember: if your love-life has been going rather badly of late, remember what was said in the chapter on BALANCE. If your pendulum of love has been swinging towards the direction of loneliness...it will only be a matter of time before it swings back to the direction of companionship and love! Once it is there, remember to *EQUILIBRATE* the forces by using *The Triangle of Manifestation* so that you do not experience another swing in the opposite direction.

CREATING WITH THE LIGHT

There is an infinite light that permeates and penetrates the entire universe. This light is the pure source of all energy and materialization. It is the primal substance which underlies all manifest existence. *The Way of Power* uses this light to enable us to work as co-creators along with the Divine.

We begin by visualizing a spiraling, zig-zagging ball of brilliant white light speeding towards us from the sky. As it approaches, we catch it in our hand. (I suggest you do all this with your eyes wide open). Toss the ball a little in front of you and see it gradually take the shape of your desire—a new car, house, vacation, television, lover, coat, and the rest.

Become like a sculptor of light. Construct in your mind's eye your desire out of the light. Then, while the form is still pliable, draw out from it strings of light leading from the form to yourself. Attach these cords of light to your body.

MAGICK ON FOOT

When you are in the process of searching for what you desire—be it a job hunt, a search for a mate, car shopping, whatever your goal may be—go with an awareness of the Tao.

Don't go out as an individual trying to wrestle some bounty from an unyielding world. That is the way of the *hard* mind—a mind that is inflexible.

Instead, go out and sense the subtle movements of the Tao. To the degree that *your* desire harmonizes with the will of the Tao, to that degree you will be successful.

There are subtle paths and patterns in the Tao. Some call these patterns the "Way of the Wyrd." Learn to see these paths in your environment. Go with the flow of the Tao.

One way to do this is to move in a gentle, but direct way. Adopt an attitude of detached exploration. Let your intuitions and subtle feelings guide you rather than your fears. The best way to shift your focus off your fear is to give up all expectation of result; be in the moment, and detach yourself emotionally from any anticipated results. Think of yourself as an explorer or adventurer of human relations.

Ride the wave of the Will of the Tao to your desired goal. When you are in synch with the Tao, it is not just you who wants the goal, but all of creation wants to match you up with this goal. Try not so much to force your desire as to *discover* your role in the Whole. Be an expression of the Tao rather than a tiny ego trying to forcibly change the world.

A FRIENDLY
ADMONITION

It is important to stop for a moment here and note that it is never appropriate to desire something that belongs to someone else, or to visualize a person doing something against their will.

For instance, if we want to find a mate, it is improper to visualize the light taking the shape of someone you know. Love should be freely given and freely received. To make someone love you against their will can incur great karmic debt.

And then there's the fact that you will need to constantly pour huge amounts of energy into keeping that person with you, if they of their own nature and accord do not wish to be with you.

Magickians who seek to dominate, abuse, and exploit the free will of others often end up depleted, burned-out shells of their former selves, because when this kind of magick is practiced an *enormous* amount of energy must be constantly exerted in order to *control* the other person.

Love is magick and you can't magick magick! So visualize your ideal mate, but create him/her from scratch; and don't try to coerce anyone you know. Besides, you may be entirely wrong in your supposition that the person you want is the right person for you...why don't you let the universe find the right person for you?

BODILY FIELDS

When you focus your attention on any part of the universe you immediately affect that part of the universe. Let's take a closer look at the many intertwined domains in the universe.

This physical world in which we dwell is but one of many interpenetrating "levels" that we humans exist upon. These so-called "levels" are in actuality interconnected energy fields.

Our very beings are made up of interwoven bodies of various types of energy, e.g., etheric, astral, ideational. These interwoven bodies are drawn from the fabric of these various energy fields.

Each of these bodies is necessary to express the qualities of a particular field. For instance, we have a *desire* body to interact with the world of emotion. We have a *mental* body to interact with the world of ideas.

These "bodies of energy" in total make up what is called the *aura*. The aura is a radiance or halo of colored lights observed by some sensitive or psychic individuals around the body.

We human beings are made up of seven bodies of energy. In addition, there are also seven fields of energy in the universe within which our human bodies of energy manifest. Each of the human being's seven bodies of energy exist and interact on its corresponding plane of universal energy. The seven bodies of energy that go to make up the human being are as follows:

1. PHYSICAL. This is our actual "skin and bones." To function in the world we must fist possess a vehicle made

of its material. (The *physical* body is also known as the *dense* body).

2. ETHERIC. The etheric body supports the health of the physical body; it is the template or blueprint of our physical heritage; it controls basic life-sustaining functions. The physical body uses the *etheric* body as its matrix and is an exact copy, molecule for molecule, of the *etheric* body. All through our lives the *etheric* body is the builder and restorer of the physical organism. This body constantly fights against the death of the *physical* body. (The *etheric* body is also known as the *subtle* body).

3. ASTRAL. In this realm is found all our emotions, our likes and dislikes, impulses, fears, passions, fantasies. When we dream we are viewing images coming to us from out of the *astral* realm; and when we drift off into reverie or fantasize we are also entering into the *astral* realm. Intense visualization and imagination take place in this field. (The *astral* body is also known as the *desire* body, or the *Sentient Soul*).

4. MENTAL. This is the realm of pure thought; here we engage in all sorts of analysis, study, opinions, viewpoints, investigation, and so forth. (The *mental* Body is also known as the *ego*).

5. PSYCHIC. The Psychic Body has the ability to perceive phenomena beyond the grasp of the physical five senses. This form of perception is known as supersensible or extra-sensory perception.

6. KARMIC. This body is connected to the infinite rebounding and echoing through-out the cosmos of the results of our thoughts and actions.

7. COSMIC. Through this aspect of ourselves we have a direct connection to the Ultimate Source of our Beings. We can contact this aspect of ourselves when we go into the SILENCE.

The first four bodies correspond to the four elements: *Earth: physical body; Water: etheric body; Fire: astral body;* and *Air: mental body.*

Advanced psychics have the ability to 'see' these planes of existence with supersensible vision. Each of these planes interpenetrate one another, and interact with one another. For instance the MIND body may want to send a message to the nerves in the legs of the PHYSICAL body, but if the ETHERIC body is weak or damaged that message will not arrive.

One of the esoteric explanations of the cause of aging is that as one gets older the body loses ETHERIC energy. At approximately thirty-five years of age the ETHERIC body begins to weaken and consequently the PHYSICAL body is adversely effected. There are many ways to strengthen the etheric forces. The ETHERIC body is directly affected by habit. For example, by teaching oneself to shave with the secondary hand rather than with the dominant one, the ETHERIC body is strengthened. Any other ambidextrous training is useful here: from brushing the teeth to learning to throw a ball with your secondary hand. The ultimate application of this technique is when individuals teach themselves to write with the non-dominant hand (geniuses and anal retentives may try writing backwards and upside down in Latin).

None of the above mentioned domains are to be taken literally as demarcations with obvious boundaries. The universe is much too graceful, fluid, and intricately woven together to fit into neat little categories. I recommend that the reader consider the occult view of the aspects of existence in a poetic way, letting the awareness of these energy fields grow as a soul-feeling in one's heart rather than cold facts cluttering up the old brain.

CREATING
THOUGHT-FORMS

Everything physical has a "spiritual" counterpart that exists on several of these planes simultaneously. There is a saying attributed to Hermes Trismegistus: "As above so below, and as below so above."

In *The Way of Power* we utilize this wisdom by creating a "thought-form" (some people call it an "astral counterpart") on these various spiritual planes. This "thought-form" will act as a seed that will manifest finally on the Physical Plane.

What is a thought-form? A thought-form is a mental creation which gains its form on one or more of the seven planes of existence, and operates there as a beacon or magnet which draws to itself similar forces. There it tends to call into activity its likeness on the physical plane!

For instance if we create a love-beacon, then it will work on the Physical Plane to draw situations and people to ourselves which will result in a love experience. "Thought-forms" are built up by a combination of raised energy (from the physical body) and concentration/visualization.

Hermes' maxim: "As above so below, and as below so above," holds much meaning for us, for it reminds us that everything here on the earth is but a small replica of that which exists on the other spiritual planes of existence.

THE COMPLETE WAY OF POWER

RESONANCE

Resonance is a term that has to do with *vibration*. To resonate means to vibrate at the same frequency as another vibrating body.

If you have two tuning forks that are both tuned to "middle C" and then you strike the first tuning fork, the second will begin to vibrate in sympathetic response to the first tuning fork!

This display of a scientific principle has great significance for our magickal work. It is an esoteric and a scientific principle that in order to cause *large* changes in a structure, one only needs to raise a *small* amount of energy, but the energy raised must vibrate at the same rate as the structure one is seeking to influence.

So you don't need to raise enormous amounts of energy, but what you *do* have to do is carefully match the frequency of the energy you raise to the frequency of the object you wish to effect.

We will now explore specific means to raise energy that resonates at the vibrational frequency of your goals.

NON-LOCAL RESONANCE

Non-local resonance is a state of being. It happens when we focus our awareness outside of ourselves in a *universal* way, as opposed to focusing inside on our internal thoughts. When we think about what we want for dinner, we resonate locally because we are thinking specifically about our needs; when we take a walk in the park thinking

126

of nothing in particular, but enjoying the grandeur of nature, we resonate non-locally.

When we resonate non-locally we attune our minds and entire being to vibrate at the frequency of something greater than ourselves, an entire *field of possibility*. We encompass a greater scope within our beings when we attune ourselves to such energies.

The majesty of a sunset, or a star-lit night sky, raises our consciousness out of our day-to-day mundane thoughts, to embrace the grand sweep and larger purpose of nature. This operation actually changes your life-wave-patterns and aligns your vibrations with the vibrations of nature. It *cleanses* you of the discordant and disharmonious fixated thinking of mundane day-to-day life.

Synchronize your being with the vibration of nature. The best place to do this is at a park, beach, forest, and so on, where one's mind can resonate non-locally with the forces of nature.

Remember, our goal in *The Way of Power* is to use the power of nature to help us energize our visualizations. We are not fighting the current, but instead plugging into the current of natural forces. When we become aware of our environment, we begin to become *One* with the energies that are present in the environment.

Step 1: Begin by Unfocusing the Mind

There are several basic steps to *The Way of Power*.

Begin by generating a state of mind in which you lose focus on yourself, a state of mind in which you lose your subjectivity.

This can be done in a quiet way through meditation on a mantra, gazing at a candle flame, looking at a yantra, focusing on one's breathing, and so on.

Again, the goal is to shift the focus off of ourselves thereby losing subjectivity.

This aim can also be achieved in a more vigorous way through ecstatic dancing, drumming, sexual intercourse, vigorous exercise, chanting, ecstasy breathing, marathon running, masturbation, and so forth, for an extended length of time...at least twenty minutes and probably about two hours ideally.

This un-focused state of undifferentiated awareness is the magickal state of mind. The magickian is not focused on any specific thing, his or her ordinary thought processes are stopped. The magickian becomes part of the great flow of existence. For in this state a person becomes attuned with the world around them.

The manipulative, overly focused mind, is hard and brittle and does violence to the matrix. It can cause some results but they are temporary and require much energy to sustain.

Our goal is to forget and abandon what we fix our attention to on a daily basis. The theory behind this is that through meditation, sex, exercise, and so forth, we reach a state of "no-mind" (sometimes referred to as *The Silence*) in which *all* possibilities exist simultaneously.

Further techniques that are useful to distract the mind and to disassociate are: burning incense, wearing costumes and masks, and ritualistic body painting.

EFFECTING CHANGE THROUGH NON-LOCAL EVENTS

Emptying the mind is a pre-requisite for successful magickal realization. A "non-local" event is defined as: one event happening in response to another event with no material or energy contact between the two. It sounds as if we were talking about magick here, but this is one of the latest 'discoveries' of quantum physics. Physicists have formulated the theory and proven in experiment that the two events are connected by a kind of underground-reality system. So we can affect people and events miles distant from us. There is solid scientific evidence to back up this assertion. Emptying the mind prepares the mind to work in a 'non-local' way.

MUSIC

Music is another method which can free us of the mental fetters which hinder our magickal operations. Music shuts down mental chatter by immersing us in the world of sound. It triggers fresh ways of knowing, turning on long dormant processes of understanding the world.

As you let go and let the music take over, your mind begins to resonate with the frequency of the music.

When the mind is attuned and plugged into the musical archetypes, resonating in a non-local way, you can safely begin the next step in our *The Way of Power* process.

Step 2: Concentrate on the Force
You Want to Bring Into Your Life

Only after you have attuned your mind to the energies around you do you begin to think more specifically. You still haven't reached the point where you focus directly on your goal.

Your task at this point is to focus on the general category into which your goal falls. You begin resonating with the specific type of energy that you want to attract into your life.

You now have *three* options, choose whichever one is most attuned to your spiritual orientation:

1. Center your awareness on Platonic concepts such as: *beauty, strength, wisdom, love, awareness, understanding,* and so on, choosing the one that pertains to your wish. For instance, if you are going to run a marathon, you might choose at this point to meditate on the concept of *strength, speed,* or *determination*. This will attune you to that specific energy.

2. Those more Shamanistically oriented can dwell on specific animal totems that personify the forces that you wish to bring into your life like: *lion, wolf, bear, deer, moose,* and so on. Perhaps, still using our marathon example, you would picture to yourself a running *deer* or *cheetah,* and actually become one with the animal as it runs through the forest.

3. Or you may choose to concentrate on a God or Goddess, from any of the world's religious pantheons that personify your goals.

Begin by procuring books of Gods and Goddesses from the various religious pantheons of the world, for instance: Greece, India, Ireland, Africa, and so forth. Look through these books and see if you can find a particular deity that corresponds with just the force you are seeking to invoke into your life. Try to find one that is particularly attractive to you and fires your imagination.

Now I am going to reveal an extremely forceful magickal technique used by Ceremonial Magickians and Ancient Shamans that you can use to empower your visualization. It is called: *assuming the "god-form" of the God or Goddess.*

To assume a "God-form" you first study all the characteristics of the God/dess you picked out as your favorite. Go back to your book and note the way they dress, stand, what they carry, their gestures, in short how the deity is conventionally portrayed.

Then reread the legends written in your book about that particular God/dess. Really familiarize yourself with their story. It may be helpful to actually tell the story to some friends (do *not* reveal to them that you are doing magick, just tell them that you enjoyed this story and want to share it with them).

This powerfully attunes the practitioner to just those forces exemplified by the deity. If you can, find a painting, poster, drawing, trading card of your hero/ine. Hang this on your wall. Do not be afraid to embrace *any* being that appeals to you. Try Comic Book characters, Super-Heros, Demons, and Fantastic Creatures for your "God-Form."

For example, a person whose goal is to win a marathon, might do well to vividly picture the Winged Goddess of Victory Nike in his or her mind, and then, as if one were putting on a mask or costume, actually draw the "God-form" over oneself, in effect becoming the Deity of Victory—Nike. The person could then imagine him or herself as Nike running the race.

If you want to find love you might assume the "God-form" of Venus or Aries. If you want to become more wise, a better speaker, and quick-witted you could invoke Mercury.

In practicing any of the three options you are attuning yourself to the energy centers within the web. Through this method you are connecting your mind and being directly to these power centers.

Step 3: Focus And Envision

Continue to become even more specific and fix your concentration on your specific goal. Powerfully picture your target in vivid and accurate detail. This creates a blueprint of your goal in the spirit worlds and this blueprint will function as the *unconscious realization* of your wants and desires.

Step 4: Raise Energy

It's now time to vitalize and energize the picture in your mind! Begin to raise energy by intoxicating the senses. Imagine drawing back a bow and aiming an "energy" arrow at your goal.

You can raise energy through trance dancing, ecstatic drumming, sexual intercourse, vigorous exercise, running, masturbation, chanting, and so forth. Whatever method you choose, do it while focusing very clearly on your target.

After you have built up a large charge of energy inside yourself, you need to liberate that energy. At the apex of arousal release the arrow of your intent into the bull's-eye of your visualization!

See all the energy you have raised flow with one sharp flight into the goal. See yourself firing "photon-torpedoes" into the image of your desire. This can be done by a loud shout at the peak of ecstasy, slapping your hands together, rapping on the walls, stamping your feet, hitting something with a stick, or with one last burst of speed or power.

This sends energy to the spiritual schematic. You are actually feeding your blueprint energy and making it come alive in the spirit realms.

Step 5: Disconnect

Pay very close attention to the following point: after sending out the energy, *let go of it completely.*

Remove your mind entirely from your target!

I strongly suggest that you not interfere with the vibrations you have set up. For in the spirit world you can cause your arrow to fly off target if you think about its flight after you have released it from the bow!

Thank the various Platonic Ideas, Totem Animals, God/desses for their help. This will enable you to formally disconnect from the power centers.

After thanking the Powers do not think about, or talk about *The Way of Power* for twenty-four hours. One of the most powerful inducements to magick is to change the mood as quickly as possible. Tell a joke, turn on the lights, eat a candy-bar, sprinkle on some perfume, change your clothes, and so forth.

If you believe you are a Magickian, then act like one. Have faith in your workings and do not dwell on them and second guess yourself.

IMPORTANCE OF FORGETTING

The practitioner of *The Way of Power* should not allow him or herself to dwell on his or her wishes.

The only times that contemplation on one's goals is permitted would be those times specifically devoted to *The Way of Power* work. At all other times consciousness of the desire should be repressed and one should strive to deliberately forget it.

In this way the desire becomes alive on the subconscious plane and eventually becomes organic. It is akin to planting a seed. A person doesn't plant a seed in a pot and the next day dig it up to see if it's growing.

The seed needs to be forgotten in the warmth and darkness of the soil. It must be allowed to germinate on its own. Digging the seed up and exhorting it to grow will only succeed in killing the seed and throwing away any hope for a plant.

SUMMARY OF THE WAY OF POWER METHOD
1. Non-Local Resonance
2. Concentrate on the Force you want to bring into your life
3. Focus and Envision
4. Raise Energy
5. Disconnect

SIGILS

WHAT IS A SIGIL?

A sigil is a symbol. It is a pattern that can represent to the subconscious mind your desired goal.

What is its practical magickal potential? A sigil can release the long dormant energies contained within the self. Through working with the sigil you can bring to waking manifestation anything contained in the various levels of the subconscious.

It can animate any archetypal force lying latent within you.

It is a powerful tool in the hands of the serious practitioner of *The Way of Power* .

There are a variety of ways that a sigil may be created. I will suggest a few of them here in this book, but the most important fact to be remembered in working with sigils is that a person should bring his or her own creativity and inventiveness to the process of creating and working with them.

TWO CHOICES

One can either use sigils to access a force or principle such as: *strength, beauty, grace, speed, aggressiveness, wisdom, sexuality*, and the rest, or sigils can be used to acquire specific goals such as: *a lover, money, stereo, clothes, house, success on an exam or test, a new contract, a raise*, and so on.

ALPHABETICAL SIGIL

We being our study of sigils with an analysis of the Alphabetical Sigil.

First, write out a one sentence statement of your desired goal, all in capital letters. Make it as succinct as possible.

If we want to access a force or power we may write something like this: I DESIRE THE GRACE OF A GAZELLE. Or if we want a specific goal we might write: I WANT A NEW CAR.

I WANT A NEW CAR.

Second, we look at the sentence and then remove all repeated letters as follows: "I WANT A NEW CAR." We are then left with the letters: I, W, A, N, T, E, C, R.

I W A N T E C R

Third, our task now involves some creativity, for we must combine these letters into a geometrical pattern of some sort. We connect all the letters into a glyph, intertwining the letters so that they are each attached to another in some way.

Fourth, we condense the entire sigil into one recognizable form. The condensed version must by simple enough for you to memorize and be able to visualize easily. With practice, the whole process becomes quite easy and fun.

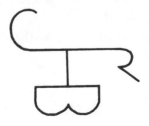

ORGANIC SIGIL

Another type of sigil I call the Organic Sigil. In this case, we first draw a very simple picture of our desired goal. If you want a house, draw a house, if you want a car, draw a car, and so forth. Let's use the example of a house.

After we have completed our drawing, we then look for one or two of the most important features of our drawing.

We then use those one or two elements from our sketch to create the sigil; the subconscious can fill in the rest.

So look for anything that stands out in the picture, a curve, a wavy line, shading, an intersection of two lines, and so on. In other words, reduce the picture to its simplest constituent parts and then select the most important element.

Remember there is no right or wrong here. Whatever stands out to you, whatever strikes you as the essence of the picture is what I want you now to notice.

Then condense the picture, ridding it of any superfluous lines, down to its most basic essence.

UTILIZING THE SIGIL

Now that we have created our sigil, we can incorporate it in our *Way of Power*. Whenever during the course of a day we are tempted to begin "wishing" for our goal, we will instead call up to mind the image of the sigil.

Concentration on a sigil serves the function of distracting the mind so that it does not analyze the goal or debate its value. This will have the effect of quieting the mind down with all its "wishing" and will instead allow the image of the sigil to sink down deep into the subconscious.

The sigil is the guiding star by which you can help steer the great ship of life to your goal.

After a while, the conscious mind will have entirely forgotten what the sigil represents and then it will be a pure subconscious key to unlocking super-powers!

Your sigil becomes a powerful machine that stimulates physical plane reorganization by gathering up and concentrating psychic forces around and within you.

CANDLE MAGICK

A powerful means to utilize sigils is to inscribe the sigil on a candle. The more deeply you cut the sigil into the wax the better. As the candle burns, the sigil is transmuted by the flame, disappearing to our conscious awareness, but reappearing and becoming animated in the spirit realm.

FOOD MAGICK

Inscribe on a piece of food your sigil. You can carve it on a piece of fruit, draw it on a loaf of baking bread, or outline it on a baking cookie.

Through the act of inscribing your magickal symbol on the food you are impregnating the food with your magickal *intention*. Then ingest the food! This technique is a direct way for a person to become *one* with their intent!!!

When you eat your sigil, you are actually causing it to become part of your body. The Word becomes flesh!

TALISMANIA

The most effective and powerful technique I could possibly share with you involves a use of sigils utilizing some extraordinarily potent principles of manifestation.

Every culture has had unique objects to be worn or held for the purpose of healing and protection. These "power objects" are known as talismans. Because of powers attributed to the materials and symbols that go into their making, talismans are a materialization of healing and life - enhancing energies.

As I have noted already, when we visualize our desires we make an impression on the astral plane. This impression is an "energy matrix" which then works invisibly to draw to us what we want.

In the Tarot card *The Wheel Of Fortune*, we see a wheel with three concentric circles. The inner circle is the creative idea, the middle is the developmental astral substance, and the outer is the physical world. Our ideas make an impression on the developmental astral substance and are then manifest in the physical world.

The point at which people's magick breaks down is that they are successful in making the impression in the astral substance, but they fail to ground the energy.

There exists a way to powerfully anchor this "energy matrix" in the physical world, a way to give the force a physical reality.

An ancient definition of the word matrix is *womb*. A matrix is a place or enveloping element within which something originates, takes form, and develops.

When I refer to an "energy-matrix" on the astral, I am pointing out that the astral world acts as a kind of *womb* -

like environment. This environment nurtures and cultivates the desire which we have embedded in this astral substance through *The Way of Power*.

The worlds of visible things are born as from a *yoni*. The *Great Unmanifest* is like a *womb*.

However, the word matrix has an additional meaning. Webster's New Collegiate Dictionary (G. & C. Merriam & Co., 1958) defines it thus: that which gives form, origin, or foundation to something enclosed or embedded in it, as a mold for casting; the natural material in which any metal, fossil, crystal, or gem is embedded.

HOW TO CREATE A TALISMAN

First create a *sigil* as explained earlier. Then obtain some modeling clay. Look for the kind that dries in the open air or in the oven.

With the clay in your hands proceed through the various steps outlined above:

1. *Non-local resonance.*
2. *Concentrate on the force you want to bring into your life.*
3. *Focus and envision.*
4. *Raise energy.*
5. *Disconnect.*

However, as you perform step four, I want you to gather up and send the psychic energy into the clay. As you reach the peak of excitement, let loose your accumulation of power into the talisman. Another way to do this is to inscribe into the clay your sigil at the exact moment of climax!

You have now taken the image of your desire (the sigil) and have driven it deeply into the clay matrix. This impregnation of the matrix has created a talisman on the physical plane.

TALISMANIA is the Art of Fixating the Volatile.

What you have created is a living being of sorts, a kind of beacon in the physical world, that will magnetically attract to you the goals and experiences you want.

Clay is representative of the element of Earth and so is very appropriate for this technique of "anchoring" the Sigil on the Physical Plane.

Those of you who are familiar with etching, carving, and metal work, can also create powerful "Talismans" using the same procedure as outlined above, but instead of clay you would utilize wood, metal, or any other natural substance.

Now carry this Spirit-Seed around with you in a pouch or put it in some sacred space. At certain regular intervals send more energy to the talisman. Periodically re-energize it, just as you would keep a plant watered regularly.

THE GROUND IS
WHERE IT'S AT

Since grounding concerns itself with anchoring something onto the physical plane or sending energy into the earth, it would not be inappropriate to mention here an example from the world of natural science. Specifically I am referring to *electrical grounding*.

Consider a lightning bolt. As you look at the sky and see storm clouds approaching, they are bouncing against one another and building up a large negative charge. This charge *wants* to go somewhere and until it does, it just continues to build up. At some point it has enough energy to make a jump! It "seeks" a place with a large positive charge and then picks the easiest path to travel to this place. This jump is what you see as lightning when the energy leaps from the negative cloud to the positive ground.

Lightning is essentially giant static electricity. Now, when the energy in the cloud has built up to a point of eruption, it seeks the nearest point that will conduct the electricity to the ground. That's why you don't want to be in an open field during a thunderstorm. You would be the nearest point to the cloud.

Electricity will always flow towards the closest ground. That's what happens when you short circuit an appliance. The electricity finds a quicker way to ground itself rather than flow through the appliance.

Consider how this physical science may be applied to *The Way of Power*. First, we understand that in the physical world a bolt of lightning will flow if it has a place to flow towards! And it will always pick the quickest path to the earth.

Therefore, to practice *The Way of Power* at an optimum level, we must provide a physical ground to which our spiritual energies can flow. We need to secure these forces onto the earth plane. Our ship of dreams must be anchored, or else it will float away!

LIGHTNING RODS

A lightning rod is used so that lightning will strike the rod rather than the building. It works because it is the highest point in the vicinity. Recall that lightning always seeks the quickest and easiest path to the ground; if you have a tall piece of metal (i.e., a conductor) going from the building to high in the air, then this is a path where the lightning would be most likely to go.

In other words, lightning will strike the rod and the energy will travel down the wire connected to the rod and end up in the earth.

We can draw wisdom from this illustration from the natural world to help us in our *Way of Power* operations. Have you ever felt that when you were really needy, everyone around you seemed to have exactly what you didn't have and seemed to be so happy and content?

When you desire a goal intensely you set up an opposing charge in your environment. When a person is desperate for love, affection, or some possession, s/he induces a charge of opposite polarity in the people and environment around him or her. This causes the people not to want to give love, or the desired property. The environment becomes more unyielding the more you want something!

When we consciously walk around feeling needy we cause others to withdraw their favors from us. This is why we should make our desires unconscious through sigils and by deliberately forgetting *The Way of Power* working after we do it.

If we walk around feeling intense desire for something, our environment will tend to close up and withhold our desires from us.

If you desperately want people to give you love, affection and the things you want, you will create the reverse feeling in the people around you. They will want to withhold their love, affection, and possessions.

Wanting people to give to you will cause people to hold on to what they've got.

How do we prevent the opposing force of the force we are invoking from building up in our environment?

Well, we must take a little closer look at the lightning bolt. Just at the instant that the energy is about to be transmitted, a small electrical herald is sent forth that goes from air to ground and a similar bit is sent from ground to the air. If they meet in the middle, then when they touch there is the main whoosh of lighting going from the cloud to the ground which we see.

So the lesson here is that before a large amount of energy is transmitted, there is always a small tentative "hello" signal that is sent forth. One signals the other. It's like flirting—each time a person signals the other, say with a smile or a wink, they are reaffirming their choice.

Therefore, be close to the action. Lightning seeks the most simple and uncomplicated path to discharge itself. So if you wish that someone give something to you, and you sense they are ready to give it, then be near as possible to them! Be where the action is. Be where the person, money, or energy that you want is!

Now, some people call this signal, a "hand-shake" signal. If someone needs a helping hand across the street, you are of no use if you're in another part of town. Likewise, just standing on the street-corner next to the person in need of help will not connect up the two of you. One of you must send out a signal, a small precursor, that you want to connect. For instance, the person in need of assistance might smile at you and you signal back by asking "May I help you across the street?" Other precursors are: floral arrangements, a letter of introduction, a business card, business attire and special jewelry.

If it is love you seek the solution lies in *accepting* love. In other words, instead of looking this way and that for someone who you can meet, you would simply walk down the street taking in whatever signs or evidence of people's caring for you.

If someone holds a door for you, lets you merge into traffic, smiles at you, or says hello, accept these things as love coming towards *you*! Allow yourself to be loved. When you take what people give you, you set up a flow in your direction.

This establishes a flow of love current in your direction. When you walk around *accepting* love you set up the opposite polarity in the people around you causing them to want to *give* love! *Behold! I give unto you a new commandment: As you receive so shall it be given unto you*.

I *strongly* recommend that you pause when something good happens to you and WAIT at least 5-10 seconds and really FEEL the pleasant sensations. Let the FEELING SINK IN! Magnetize yourself with the feeling of pleasure!

The next step is to develop a feeling of warmth and affection for small things. This will cause your love vibrations to radiate out from you. Be a friend and you will have friends. Genuinely care about people. If you don't feel any warmth towards your fellow human beings, then I doubt very much if you really have all that much love to give. But let the tides of give and take, serve and served, care-giver and care-receiver, aggressive and passive, to wash over you and breathe in and out of your soul.

THE CADUCEUS OF HERMES AS PORTRAYAL OF THE TRIANGLE OF MANIFESTATION

The serpent is a symbol known to the Celts, Voodooists, Thelemites, Tantrics and the ancient faiths of Asia and Egypt. The serpent represents *wisdom, silence* and *reproductive energy*. It is associated symbolically with the interplay of time and life.

In the Caduceus, the two serpents are called *Ob* and *Od*. As they twine around each other, they create the magickal wand of Double Power. The unification of the Ob and Od is pictured by the *globe* that crowns the Caduceus.

The globe which climaxes the Caduceus symbolizes the *Nur Muhammadi*, or Light of Mohammed, the *Aur* (Light) in Hebrew, which is the *result* of the state of equilibrium existing between the two serpent forces.

This Light is the SUPREME ESSENCE. Wilhelm Reich called this serpent energy the *Orgone*. It has also been referred to as: Ki, Kundalini, Mana, Prana, Vril, Animal Magnetism, the Odic Force, the astral light, the *élan vital*, the *libido*, the Atmospheric 'I' and Ether.

SERPENT MAGICK

The serpent represents the universal force. This power is the very force that moves the universe. Behind all phenomena lies this serpent force. An African creation myth has the great serpent's seven thousand coils setting the stars and planets in motion. Serpent brought life to Earth and still can be seen moving in the current of a river, vaulting over us in the form of the rainbow and blazing down within the lightning.

According to Greek mythology, at the origin of the world existed the Goddess Rhea. Her son Zeus in serpent-form coupled with his mother, who was also serpentine at the time. The great Odin disguised himself as a serpent, as did Loki; this parallels Zeus as the 'good serpent' (*Agathos daimon)* and Typhon as the 'evil serpent' (*Kakos daimon*).

In certain mythologies, Gods and Goddesses would actually wear serpents around their bodies. In Celtic mythology Ceneu Menrud ('red mark') kept a serpent about his neck for a year; Conal Cearnach, *of the Victories*, had a serpent-creature coiled around his waist which served him in battle in the *Tain Bo Fraoch*; Carados correspondingly had a serpent wrapped around his arm.

The Druid of the Welsh Triads exclaims in ecstatic trance: "I am a serpent!" Ancient Ireland was certainly given to Serpent Worship and the traditions seems to have continued well into the Common Era. The Milesian Celts would carve a snake twisted around a rod. The Crozier, or Pastoral Staff of Cashel, which was found in the 19th Century, bears a serpent springing out of a sheath or vagina. At Clonmel, there is a cross having four serpents at the center, coiled round a spherical boss. Several instances have been known in which the serpents have been more or less chipped away from off such crosses.

Medusa, as Moon and Earth Goddess, was conveyed in a serpent-drawn chariot. The Book of John 3:14-15 states: "Even as Moses lifted up the Serpent in the Wilderness, even so must the Son of Man be lifted up, that everyone who believes in him may have eternal life."

SERPENTINE ECSTASIES

Communion is any act of mutual intercourse, especially intimate intercourse. Communion is also the reception of something from the Divine: the something that IS the Divine. When one 'takes' communion, one is having intimate intercourse with the Divine.

Conceive of your spine as being a serpent. Then think of your skull as a bowl of divine nectar or spirit-energy. Visualize the serpent as lapping up the nectar out of the base of the vessel. The serpent is receiving the communion from the bowl. It is as if the spine were the phallus and the valley of the skull, the yoni. Perfect communion, perfect equilibrium and balance inside yourself!

Visualize a small serpent as coming out of the front of your skull. Its tail rests in the base of your brain and its head looks straight forward out from your skull. Now open your 'serpent' eyes and look out into the spirit world. You can channel energy out of your brain through this fashion.

THE SERPENT LIGHTNING ROD

We know that behind every physical effect in this universe is a real, but invisible, spiritual force. For instance, a plant's growth is directed by its etheric body. Even seemingly lifeless objects, such as stones, are really living spiritual beings and are produced by spiritual forces weaving a web of manifestation in the mineral domain.

So, it is not surprising that human-made physical objects can not only affect the physical world, but also affect the spirit realms.

Our goal then is to create a serpent "lightning-rod" that we will use to manifest our wishes on the earth plane and to neutralize undesirable opposing forces in our environment.

First, visualize your Serpent Lightning Rod in the Astral World. In other words, for several weeks work out in your *imagination* exactly how you want this rod to look. The Rod is the mundane representation of the Serpent. It should be at least as tall as your waist. Conceive of the Serpent Lightning Rod on the astral, so that it has its foundation in the spirit realms. It is not necessary to make the Rod *look* like a serpent. It is important that the Rod look like the image you visualize in the Astral. You can take an appropriate size stick of wood and paint on it an image of a serpent entwining itself around the stick. Wood need not be the only substance used or the main one for that matter. The only requirement is that substance be a conductor for energy—for this purpose a crystal, wood, or metallic staff or pole would all suffice.

The Serpent Lightning Rod is the most powerful magickal tool because it manifests *The Triangle of Manifestation* on the physical plane. The Serpent consolidates both polarities in perfect balance and unity. The Serpent is an ancient symbol of the Earth Spirit. The Serpent has a solar/masculine/phallic quality. It also shares the nature of the Earth Spirit in that the serpent is self-generating through the shedding of its skin.

The Serpent Lightning Rod represents the essence of the Magickal energy of the Earth commingled with the essence of the Magickal energy of the Sun.

Plant your Rod firmly in the ground in broad daylight. Let the sun's rays play on the serpent-pole. In your mind's eye, envisage the pole as an arrow of energy penetrating the receptive target of the Earth. Your Serpent Lightening Rod is a bolt of flame from Heaven. You are holding the primary dynamism, the Uplifted Rod of Power! It is the Phallus, the virile member at its most potent. You grasp pure being in your hands.

Lay your Rod down on the ground at night under the soft light of the Moon and silver Stars. See the Moon shoot forth a ray and watch it gently land on the Earth. The ray transforms itself into your Serpent Lighting Rod. Reflect on how a serpent will periodically shed its skin and emerge transformed, gleaming and more beautiful than before!

You are at the Center of the Universe. You connect Earth to Sky, Sky to Earth.

Can psychic and etheric energies be broken up when they present a barrier to our achieving our goals?

The Serpent Lightning Rod exists as a bridge between the worlds. When you take it out and work with it you are balancing the energies within yourself and around your environment. Picture what is in disharmony in front of you and point your Rod at it. Don't try to do anything. Just let the energy flow back and forth and connect. The energy will then of its own nature reach a state of equilibrium.

The Serpent Lightning Rod equalizes the pressures between the two energy potentials. For example, the Rod could equalize the difference of potential between having no transportation and having a Mercedes Benz. The Rod could counter-balance the difference between having no friends and being surrounded by loving friends.

Wilhelm Reich demonstrated the equalizing of unbalanced energy potentials with his "cloud-buster." The *cloud-buster* dissipates clouds of water vapor by withdrawing, according to the orgonomic principle, atmospheric (cosmic) '*OR*' energy from the center of the cloud. There will then be *less* energy to carry the water vapors and the clouds necessarily dissipate. The orgonomic potential between cloud and its environment is lowered. The *OR* charges are drawn into water, preferably *flowing* water of brooks, streams, flowing lakes and rivers.

As the "cloud-buster" dissipates cloudy skies, you too can break up negative situations with your Serpent Lightning Rod. If there's tension between you and a friend, boss or lover the Serpent Lightening Rod can dispel the negative energy.

When you are sexually aroused you are building up a bio-electric charge that can be discharged through orgasm. All of biological life, according to Reich, can be seen as a function of tension and discharge. When we have accumulated enough energy charge we slam the Serpent Lightning Rod hard down on the floor. The collapse of the wave function ripples outward, changing the previous destiny that you had created, changing the rhythm of the atmosphere around you, and simultaneously discharging the energy of your desire from the rod.

Many cultures believe that *crossroads* are sacred. Indeed, crossroads are places that exist between the worlds, for in truth, where does one road lead off and the other begin? This "place between" the worlds is similar to other places on the earth: the sea-shore (not earth/not sea), the horizon (not air/not earth), the tip of a flame (not fire/not air).

When the magickal wand hits the floor it collides with the meeting point. The Rod becomes the World Tree, the very *center* round which existence doth dance. This center has also been called the *world navel*. At this meeting point, the Serpent Rod puts things together. It pulls things together which do not agree. The Secret of the Rod is that it is an equilibrant. As you hammer your scepter into the ground state out loud: "I am the center of the Earth, I am where all Cycles meet, everything begins and ends with me."

The serpent has always been connected with death for several reasons. Many serpents are poisonous and excrete deadly venom. Additionally, the serpent burrows underneath the earth, traveling through the Underworld, and re-emerges into the daylight onto the surface of the earth.

The serpent re-creates itself every time it sheds its skin. It perpetuates itself by letting the old skin drop off. We humans do this when we die. We 'shed our skins' at death, thereby allowing ourselves to continue. We drop the body behind as we slip out of the sheaths of our etheric and astral bodies. That is why the serpent is a revealer of the Mystery of Life and Death. The serpent teaches us that death is a necessary part of our existence; death does not end our existence, it permits us to continue. The serpent represents the unquenchable fire of will. It is the force that comes out of the egg. The serpent must exist in the most severe of blazing hot deserts, enduring difficult climates and jungles, and still manage to persist and continue.

It is for just this reason that the Serpent Lightning Rod enables travel through time and space at the blink of an eye. In its succession of existences, it can dance through time, as it sheds off epochs and grows new time and space coordinates.

THE MAGICKAL BUDDY

Many magickal systems recommend one work with a "magickal partner," usually a person of the opposite sex, with whom to perform various magickal rites. However, finding such a partner is not always possible, nor is it always desirable—some people *prefer* to work alone magickly.

But in my opinion, in working Magick in one's daily life there is *nothing* so valuable as a friend on the path. S/he need not be a full "magickal partner," but, at least, someone who can support you in an emotional and spiritual sense. This path can sometimes be demanding and it really helps to have a buddy with whom you can plan out your various workings and report the assorted results of your operations.

When you try to apply any discipline all by yourself, sometimes you start out with the best of intentions, but when the going gets rough, the rough get going! But, if you have a friend with whom you've shared your plans, then you are more likely to *stick* to your plan of action.

A magickal friend can support you in moments of spiritual doubt and discouragement. They can encourage you to continue with your studies and workings. They can suggest new and different approaches. They can share with you the results *they* have had in similar situations.

You may be saying to yourself: "Where can I find such a person?" It's not that hard. Place an ad in one of the Magickal, Pagan, Cyberpunk, or Rock magazines stating that you are looking for a *friend* to discuss magick with and to form a buddy-system. Put an ad up in your local occult book-store; even most personal ad sections now-a-days have sections devoted to people looking for "Friends Only." Be *very specific*. State *exactly* what kind of magick you are into, tell a little about your personal interests, state that you want to find a friend for mutual magickal support and encouragement!

Think of the excitement and pleasure of knowing that you will have someone to report all your magickal results to at the end of the day! Also, realize, that you will be more willing to do *difficult* operations when you know that you have your friend's support and confidence in you!

A support group is helpful, but even more helpful in my opinion, is *one good friend*, who is on the same wavelength as you, and with whom you can share your deepest magickal secrets.

CONCLUSION

In the Tarot card deck, *The Hermit* card intimates that our knowledge is empty and meaningless until we turn and give it to others. I have endeavored through writing this book to share with you the result of over twenty years of spiritual investigation.

I hope I have provided you with a fresh approach to imagistic magick, stripped of all the accretions of patriarchal and hierarchical theology, to fill in the gaps that are found in much Magickal literature.

I know some people may be tempted to put this book down, because they are not yet ready to begin the required work to bring their desires into materialization. They may still be locked in the battle of wanting and not-wanting their goals. A very large part of themselves doesn't want anything to change. I suggest if this applies to you to go back to the sections on "Respecting Our Inner Selves" and "Something to Think About."

Then there are those people who will prefer to wander through the fairy-tale land of superficial affirmation and positive thinking, so as not to confront other dimensions of themselves.

Like *The Fool* in the Tarot Deck, you *must* walk blindly off the cliff into the ABYSS of the UNKNOWN!

It takes great courage and character to go behind our masks and face our true selves. But this is the real task of the magickian. S/he must first transform him or herself.

It is never easy to cast off from oneself the cherished notions of childhood and it is no less easy to face the fact that in order to grow spiritually one must accept a more sophisticated world-view.

But for those who are ready to begin regular, disciplined practice, the rewards will be well worth the effort. For *The Way of Power* techniques work with Nature, in harmony with the flow of the cosmos, ultimately connecting one to the Point from which All Creation flows.

Power flows from this Point. Do not be ashamed for wanting to be *POWERFUL*. It is popularly more acceptable to use phrases similar to "feeling energetic," "send me some energy," "feel the energy flowing through you." Yet, energy is just another word for *POWER*. *POWER* brings force, strength, potency, stamina, and vigor. There is no need to steal power from others or abuse others to feel power when you are connected to the *source* from which All Creation flows.

Power is not intrinsically evil or negative, just as wind is not intrinsically evil. Power simply "is". Regarding the use of *POWER* to effect authority, domination, and control: guide oneself through awareness of the Karmic consequences of the applications of *POWER*. For the more advanced student on the path, Karma reveals itself to be a concept and, like any other concept, can only hold power over a person if that person believes in it.

A terrible responsibility settles on the shoulders of the Adept: the Adept is truly a god. If you treat people terribly then you are decreeing that the world is a place in which people are treated terribly. This can become a spiral into despair, as the world continuously reflects your own mind. Be aware of the existence you are creating around yourself, for that existence is you!

If any of your dreams can become a reality for you as they have for me, then I shall not have wasted your money and time in purchasing and reading this book.

Make no excuses for yourself. Make no excuses for wanting to have your needs met. *DOES THE FLOWER ASK PERMISSION TO BLOOM?*

As a Magickian, your task is to break the world's hold on you. I recommend that you see how, when, and where society, media, books and religion control you and live your life for you. You are being lived. Wake up to that shocking fact! And then take back your power. Don't be the puppet of any society, any occult philosophy, *ANYTHING*! Some people are truly *POSSESSED* by the culture. To thine own self be true! Choose, with intention, what direction to take with your life.

Synthesize the Two Opposites in the Point of Transcendence, and *GO BEYOND* narrow minded ways of viewing reality.

If you really think you are ready to take charge of your own life, and if you take the necessary steps outlined in this book, then you will indeed reap the rewards of *THE WAY OF POWER*. Go out and put these principles into action.

There is no reality but the Ultimate Reality; You are the Emissary of that Reality. Make life a celebration of You!

ABOUT THE AUTHOR

LAURENCE GALIAN, pianist, writer, lecturer, composer, teacher of ancient lore and modern wisdom, was born in Manhattan on April 5, 1954 (Aries, Taurus Moon, Leo Rising). He has always approached metaphysics and the spirit world with a ruthless honesty: he uses what works and discards the rest.

He began his music studies at the age of six with James Gerard DeMartini, a professor at Brooklyn College. Today he holds the full-time position of *Senior Dance Accompanist* in the *Hofstra University Department of Drama and Dance*. He has accompanied many of the greatest dancers and companies in the world including Natalia Makarova, Jennifer Muller and The Works, Joyce Trisler Danscompany, and The San Francisco Ballet. He also serves on the Faculty of the *Hofstra College of Continuing Education* where he teaches classes in: Wicca, Qabalah, Ceremonial Magick, and Welsh mythology. He has recorded a solo piano album of ballet music entitled *Ballet Music for Barre and Center Floor*, available as a double-length CD from Roper Records, Inc. His original ballet, *Zemzem*, was aired on the National Public Radio Program "New Sounds With John Schaefer." He is listed in the fifteenth edition of *International Who's Who in Music* (Cambridge, England).

He has studied metaphysics all his life. He is a professional Handwriting Analyst, Tarot Reader, Spiritual Consultant and a practicing Wiccan Priest with a special interest in Celtic Shamanism. He is a member of the *Alliance of Magical and Earth Religions, The Temple of Danann* and *New Moon New York*, a Pagan networking organization.

In 1981 Laurence met Sheikh Muzaffer Ozak and the Halveti-Jerrahi dervishes of Istanbul, Turkey. The Jerrahis practice mystical Islam (Sufism) and have an unbroken line of transmission spanning over seven hundred years. The founder of the order was Hazreti Pir Nureddin Jerrahi, The Axis of the Sufis. After a foreordained period of study, Laurence was initiated into this order in 1983.

Mr. Galian enjoys hearing from his readers. Sometimes he is available for seminars, book signings, and workshops. You can contact him at Box 297, Jericho, New York 11753-0927, U.S.A.